THE PERIODIC TABLE OF

WRITTEN BY
MELANIE SCOTT

CONTENTS

INTRODUCTION

The quest for scientific knowledge is a never-ending journey of exploration, constantly pushing at the edges of the possible. This real-world truth is seen in the pages of DC's comics, in the stories and the remarkable characters who populate them. Science has always been at the heart of the DC universe as a mechanism for the advancement of wonder, making the incredible seem achievable and within reach.

As we take steps along the path of discovery, a Multiverse is revealed, where familiar yet strange versions of beloved characters play out their differing realities. And beyond the vast Multiverse there is more to explore, out into the wider Omniverse and in the dimensions outside of space and time.

The Multiverse itself functions because of the presence of hidden forces—all-powerful entities and manifestations of governing principles. The Speed Force represents and guides the forward motion of time and reality, while the Emotional Spectrum transforms the feelings of sentient beings into energies. Certain heroes like The Flash and Green Lantern are attuned to these energies and can harness them to do great things. Another type of Multiversal energy is that of the divine or magical, occupying a space in reality known as the Sphere of the Gods and populated by godlike and mystical beings such as Wonder Woman and Zatanna.

The science of DC has also discovered new elements. The powerful "divine metals" bestow many benefits including long life, resurrection, flight, or superhuman durability. These metals attract many seeking to utilize their powers, including heroes like Hawkman and Cyborg, but also numerous villains.

In laboratories, chemical concoctions are devised to augment the abilities of otherwise ordinary humans, and the mysteries of DNA are constantly being unlocked. The scientific term for those who exhibit powers and capabilities unknown in regular people is "metahuman." While this can apply to aliens, like Superman, or those of different genotypes on Earth such as Aquaman's Atlanteans, it can also relate to a human born with

a "metagene," like Black Canary. This means that they are naturally capable of doing extraordinary things.

Yet some of the most enduring and memorable characters are the regular—yet exceptional—humans. Batman fights for justice enhanced only with his advanced technology and peerless investigative mind.

While the entities of the DC Omniverse are a rich and varied tapestry of existence, the building blocks of their characteristics can be categorized just like the periodic table of elements. This allows us to appreciate that the unique qualities of seemingly differing characters does not preclude shared experiences and commonalities between them.

HOW TO EXPLORE THIS BOOK

The Periodic Table of DC looks at the exciting and enduring mythos of the DC universe in a completely new way. Whereas previous encyclopedias have grouped characters by team affiliation or perhaps in order of appearance, this book presents them according to their most fundamental facets—the origin of their powers or abilities. Each chapter looks at a particular category, with subdivisions within it to make the "taxonomy" more focused. Within these chapters, each character featured has their own periodic table reference, comprising a unique symbol code and an "atomic number" reflecting their first appearance in relation to others within that chapter. They are further classified according to their elemental properties, their dominant behavior classified as bonding agents, combustible, reactive, stable, toxic, or volatile.

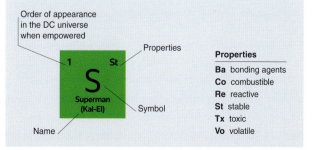

Order of appearance
in the DC universe
when empowered

Properties

1		St
	S	
Superman (Kal-El)		

Symbol

Name

Properties

Ba bonding agents
Co combustible
Re reactive
St stable
Tx toxic
Vo volatile

POWERS NOT REQUIRED

While the science of metahumans is astonishing, there is nothing more courageous than those who try and match these powerful entities armed only with their intellect, technological know-how, ingenious armor, or special weapons.

SUPERIOR TALENTS

These humans are the peak of their species, honing their natural abilities to do great things.

2 St **B** Batman (Bruce Wayne)	5 St **Ct** Catwoman	32 St **N** Nightwing	27 St **Bg** Batgirl	50 St **Bf** Batman (Jace Fox)	47 St **Bw** Batwoman	70 St **Op** Orphan	63 St **Sp** Spoiler
68 St **Bt** Batwing	62 St **Hu** Huntress	69 St **Bu** Bluebird	48 St **Ro** Robin	13 St **Af** Alfred Pennyworth	36 St **Rb** Red Robin	44 St **Hd** Red Hood	3 St **Pd** G.C.P.D.
1 St **L** Lois Lane	9 St **Ol** Jimmy Olsen	17 St **I** Iris West	30 Vo **Ls** Lady Shiva	21 Vo **Cb** Captain Boomerang	16 Vo **Dh** Deadshot	57 St **Tg** Bronze Tiger	60 Tx **Jd** Cheshire
71 St **Lh** Cheshire Cat	61 Vo **Sq** Shado	56 St **Rc** Richard Dragon	8 St **Gr** Green Arrow (Oliver Queen)	38 St **Ar** Arsenal	49 St **Rw** Red Arrow	40 St **Gw** Green Arrow (Connor Hawke)	35 Ba **Wr** Amanda Waller
26 Vo **Pc** Peacemaker	12 St **Tv** Steve Trevor	29 St **Hx** Jonah Hex	52 St **Pk** Manhunter (Paul Kirk)	58 Vo **Lv** Manhunter (Mark Shaw)	66 St **Kt** Manhunter (Kate Spencer)	53 Ba **Rf** Rick Flag Jr.	

AMAZING ARMOR AND WONDROUS WEAPONS

Some humans augment themselves with high-tech armored suits or unique weaponry.

46 St	22 St	45 St	25 St	37 St	43 St	39 St	42 St
Am	**Ap**	**Be**	**Bk**	**Sl**	**Sn**	**Sm**	**Cw**
The Atom (Ryan Choi)	The Atom (Ray Palmer)	Blue Beetle (Jaime Reyes)	Blue Beetle (Ted Kord)	Steel (John Henry Irons)	Steel (Natasha Irons)	Starman (Jack Knight)	Stargirl

34 St	19 St	4 St	11 St	31 St	18 Vo	28 Vo	15 Vo
Bo	**Ag**	**Wd**	**Jh**	**Kn**	**Cc**	**Bm**	**Ha**
Booster Gold	Adam Strange	Sandman	Guardian	Katana	Captain Cold	Black Manta	Jervis Tetch

33 Tx
Fs
Black Mask

GENIUS INTELLIGENCE

Those who are blessed with superior intellect have an advantage that can be used for good—or bad.

6 Vo	10 Vo	7 Tx	14 Vo	64 Vo	51 Vo	67 Vo	41 St
Lx	**P**	**Sr**	**Ri**	**Tc**	**Hs**	**Py**	**Mt**
Lex Luthor	The Penguin	The Scarecrow	The Riddler	Trickster	Hugo Strange	Professor Pyg	Mister Terrific

20 St	23 St	24 St	59 St	55 Vo	54 Vo	65 Vo
Rp	**Wi**	**Nc**	**Lb**	**Mw**	**Pi**	**Vc**
Rip Hunter	Will Magnus	Niles Caulder	Silas Stone	T. O. Morrow	Professor Ivo	Veronica Cale

POWERS NOT REQUIRED:
SUPERIOR TALENTS

BATMAN

2	St
B	
Batman	

REAL NAME: Bruce Wayne **POWERS/ABILITIES:** Prodigious intellect; martial arts; peak human fitness **FIRST APPEARANCE:** *Detective Comics* #27 (May 1939) **SUBSIDIARY CATEGORY:** Amazing Armor and Wondrous Weapons, Genius Intelligence, Earth Elements

Bruce Wayne is not born with a metagene giving him extraordinary powers, but nevertheless his life's path leads him to become one of the World's Greatest Super Heroes, commanding respect among his closest allies and fear among his enemies.

Born into privilege as a member of one of Gotham City's elite families, young Bruce's world is shattered when his parents are killed in a robbery gone wrong. A lonely child in the echoing Wayne Manor, he is brought up by devoted family retainer Alfred Pennyworth and develops an almost obsessive drive to bring criminals to justice, in order to prevent others from suffering the same tragedy as he has.

To this end, Bruce leaves Gotham City and travels the world, training under various masters to attain the absolute peak of human capability. He becomes skilled in a wide range of fighting techniques and martial arts, a master of disguise, a forensics expert, and a builder and designer of cutting-edge gadgetry. His natural flair for investigation—

As a man of science, Batman is most at home in the Batcave— equal parts garage, museum, research facility, surveillance hub, and laboratory.

coupled with a photographic memory—later leads him to earn the epithet "the World's Greatest Detective."

He returns home, ready to use his formidable skill set to clean up the streets and protect the ordinary citizens of Gotham City. To inspire terror in those who would harm the innocent, he harnesses one of his own fears—stemming from a traumatic experience as a child with the bats living in the caves under Wayne Manor—to create a dark alter ego: Batman.

In his mission to become the ultimate crime fighter, Batman hones his body to combat-ready perfection and uses his genius intellect to invent equipment which can aid him against the deadliest villains. His Batsuit armor is made from bulletproof material, while the cowl that hides his true identity is fitted with various add-ons to shield him from toxins and sound weapons and aid his navigation in various environmental conditions. Batman's Utility Belt can carry an array of useful mission items such as a grappling hook, breathing aids, and Batarangs, his signature bat-shaped throwing weapons.

METAL MAN

Batman discovers that he has been chosen as a conduit for the Dark Multiverse demon Barbatos to access Earth, a process that involves the Dark Knight being "mantled" with five so-called divine metals: Nth Metal, Promethium, Electrum, Dionesium, and Batmanium. The effect of Dionesium on Batman is dramatic, bringing him back to life after a fight with The Joker and erasing all of his old battle scars and even his memory. Dedicated to science and reason, Batman has reluctantly learned to accept magic as a potential part of his arsenal in certain situations. This is part of his desire to be ready for any eventuality, including the prospect of his Justice League teammates going rogue. It comes as a shock to some of them that Batman has a contingency plan to stop each Justice League member if he has to—for instance, magic would be one of the few potential weapons that might stop his close friend and ally Superman. Batman is the living embodiment of the idiom "Fail to prepare, prepare to fail ..."

CATWOMAN

REAL NAME: Selina Kyle **POWERS/ABILITIES:** Martial arts; peak human reflexes and agility; master thief **FIRST APPEARANCE:** *Batman* Vol 1 #1 (Mar 1940)

Selina Kyle is used to operating in the shadows. Formerly a master thief, when she switches to life as a hero she finds that a lot of her skills are extremely transferable. She is well-versed in the criminal mindset, and her experience planning daring heists gives her a good foundation for approaching missions in a practical way.

Growing up in a troubled home, Selina had to learn to look after herself at an early age, both physically and mentally. She loves cats, and when she is older she takes to wearing a feline-themed costume to create a new persona for herself. While Selina can sometimes struggle to cope with what life throws at her, Catwoman can take it all.

FELINE FIGHTER

Catwoman's costume is not just a look— it also contains some very useful features. Clawed gloves can be used as weapons in close combat, as well as giving more purchase when scrambling around Gotham City's buildings. She sometimes wears goggles that help her see at night and can detect security lasers—ideal for either stealing a diamond or breaking into

a crimelord's lair. Selina is also known for brandishing a whip, a multipurpose item that can be a weapon, a climbing aid, and a way of disarming opponents without having to get within arm's reach of them.

Even without weapons, Selina is a highly skilled fighter with incredible reflexes and agility, much like the animal from which she takes inspiration. While she has a history of rule-breaking and stealing from the rich, she is also fiercely protective of the downtrodden folk of Gotham City, and she will always stand up to bullies.

Catwoman can traverse the city rooftops as easily and stealthily as any feline, her dark costume helping her blend into the shadows.

NIGHTWING

REAL NAME: Dick Grayson **POWERS/ABILITIES:** Acrobatics; peak human fitness
FIRST APPEARANCE (AS NIGHTWING): *Tales of the Teen Titans* Vol 1 #44 (Jul 1984)

Mentored as a hero from an early age by Batman, who takes him in after his parents are killed, Dick Grayson learns everything there is to know about fighting crime without metahuman powers. Dick's background is in the circus, where he was one of the star performers, an acrobat of outstanding natural talent. When he becomes Robin, fighting at Batman's side, his incredible agility serves him well as he masters taking on opponents who might be physically bigger than him or armed with a weapon.

OWNING THE NIGHT

When Dick strikes out to forge his own identity, he takes the moniker Nightwing and adopts a new, darker suit, made of bulletproof material but still flexible enough for him to move freely. He also begins to carry his own weapons, intended for nonlethal combat as Batman has always taught. Nightwing favors escrima sticks, two short staffs that can be held one in each hand. These are more powerful than they appear. They can be electrified to produce a taser effect, they carry tranquilizer darts, and they fire out wires that Nightwing can use

for swinging around the city. He also carries Wing Dings, his version of the Batarang.

As should be expected from a former protégé of Batman, Nightwing's suit conceals a wide range of gadgetry enabling him to efficiently deal with different situations, such as advanced tracking devices and small explosives.

While Dick is a brilliant acrobat and fighter, as well a master detective, he is also a natural leader, one who cares deeply about those he fights with and for. His knack of bringing people together and his warm personality have made him a pivotal member of several Super Hero teams and someone who other heroes, even the most powerful, truly look up to.

Nightwing is one of the world's finest acrobats, his supreme athleticism giving him the edge in fighting even against powerful opponents.

BATGIRL

REAL NAME: Barbara Gordon **POWERS/ABILITIES:** Martial arts; prodigious intellect; computer hacking **FIRST APPEARANCE:** *Detective Comics* Vol 1 #359 (Jan 1967) **SUBSIDIARY CATEGORY:** Genius Intelligence

Barbara Gordon may have taken up crime-fighting to emulate Batman and follow in the footsteps of her detective father, but she has forged her own unique identity in the world of costumed heroes. She is courageous, moral, and fiercely intelligent, and has faced innumerable challenges with determination.

Barbara studied ballet as a young girl, a discipline which contributes to her strength and agility as she grows. She also studies a variety of martial arts, enabling her to learn techniques for getting the better of larger and stronger opponents. However, Barbara's world is shattered when she is shot and paralyzed by The Joker. Even this terrible trauma does not stop her from fighting crime; instead, she finds a different approach. As Oracle, Barbara is a hacker and information broker, at the center of a technological hub to give vital intel to her allies in the field.

ORACLE ON THE MOVE

After using cutting-edge medical technology to regain the use of her legs, Barbara returns to action as Batgirl, although she remains heavily involved in information-gathering.

With the rest of the Batman Family to call on for the physical action, she often finds that her most important role is still as Oracle. Using her technical know-how, Barbara devises a mobile Oracle suit for herself, appearing to be civilian clothing but packed with tech for observation and more—she can even override traffic signals to speed up her journeys around the city.

Barbara Gordon's dedication to fighting crime is beyond doubt, and she will do whatever it takes to support her friends and family, and protect those that need protecting. She is the perfect blend of a formidable intellectual and a skilled fighter.

Batgirl is the protector of her local neighborhood of Burnside in Gotham City, but her activities as technological marvel Oracle mean she can have eyes and ears anywhere in the world.

BATMAN

50 **St**

Bf
Batman

REAL NAME: Jace Fox **POWERS/ABILITIES:** Martial arts; prodigious intellect **FIRST APPEARANCE (AS PRIME EARTH BATMAN):** *I Am Batman* Vol 1 #0 (Oct 2021) **SUBSIDIARY CATEGORIES:** Amazing Armor and Wondrous Weapons, Genius Intelligence

When Bruce Wayne's path takes him away from Gotham City, Jace Fox, son of Wayne Industries' tech supremo Lucius, becomes a new kind of Batman. He dons a fresh version of the Batsuit engineered from an old armored suit and created on a 3D printer. The suit's chestplate is made from non-Newtonian fluid, far thinner than standard bulletproof material but just as strong, while the gauntlets are ultra-strong graphene. The mask contains a biohazard filter to counter gases and toxins. He avoids too much tracking tech within the suit to enable him to move around the city streets with minimal observation.

BATWOMAN

47 **St**

Bw
Batwoman

REAL NAME: Kate Kane **POWERS/ABILITIES:** Martial arts; weapons training; acrobatics; prodigious intellect **FIRST APPEARANCE (OF KATE KANE AS BATWOMAN):** *52* Vol 1 #11 (Sep 2006)

Katherine "Kate" Kane is Bruce Wayne's cousin, a former soldier who takes up costumed crime fighting after she is discharged from the military. As Batwoman, she brings an elite level of training to the streets of Gotham City. Her Batsuit is designed by her father, Colonel Jacob Kane, who wants her to be as well protected as possible. The suit also protects her identity, so she can maintain her civilian life as a socialite. Like her more famous cousin, Kate is from one of Gotham City's oldest families, so she is able to finance all the weapons, equipment, and vehicles she needs to be at the top of her game.

ANCILLARY EXEMPLARS

70 **St**

Op
Orphan

63 **St**

Sp
Spoiler

68 **St**

Bt
Batwing

62 **St**

Hu
Huntress

69 **St**

Bu
Bluebird

Assassins' child **Orphan** is virtually mute, but adept at reading body language. She becomes one of the new Batgirls along with the former **Spoiler**, Stephanie Brown, also the daughter of a villain. Luke Fox uses his natural flair for creating tech, inherited from his father Lucius, to equip his state-of-the-art **Batwing** suit. **Huntress** is more low-tech in her approach, favoring a crossbow with which she is deadly accurate. Harper Row is **Bluebird**, an expert electrical engineer even though she is still just a teenager.

ROBIN

REAL NAME: Damian Wayne **POWERS/ABILITIES:** Martial arts; weaponry skills; prodigious intellect **FIRST APPEARANCE (OF DAMIAN AS ROBIN):** *Batman* Vol 1 #657 (Nov 2006) **SUBSIDIARY CATEGORY:** Genius Intelligence

The son of Batman (Bruce Wayne) and Talia al Ghūl, Damian is at first raised by his mother to join the ranks of the League of Assassins, with his father completely unaware of his existence.

His al Ghūl heritage makes Damian arrogant and unscrupulous, but when Batman discovers his son, he tries to change that by teaching him a brand new code of ethics. Damian leaves the life of an assassin behind and becomes a hero as the new Robin. Despite his youth, his intensive training has made him a deadly fighter, and he is extremely skilled with a wide range of weaponry. He is very intelligent, especially in the field of engineering, and has been taught the art of detection by the best in the business—Batman.

ALFRED PENNYWORTH

REAL NAME: Alfred Pennyworth **POWERS/ABILITIES:** Military and weapons training; espionage; medical knowledge **FIRST APPEARANCE:** *Batman* Vol 1 #16 (May 1943)

Although his job title might be "butler," Alfred Pennyworth's role in the Batman Family goes way beyond that. A father figure to the young orphan Bruce Wayne, as time goes by, Alfred also cares for the other lost young people who pass through the doors

of Wayne Manor, including all the heroes who have used the Robin alias. While Alfred's empathy with his charges may be his most distinguishing trait, he has a wealth of practical skills from his past, which include spells as a successful actor and a secret agent. Alfred is usually the one to patch up Batman when he is wounded on a mission, and he is often found at the control center of the Batcave, feeding intelligence to the Dark Knight in the field. He is always troubled when Bruce comes home injured, and has threatened to resign if he feels that Batman is endangering himself without good reason.

RED ROBIN

REAL NAME: Tim Drake **POWERS/ABILITIES:** Martial arts; formidable intellect; computer hacking **FIRST APPEARANCE (AS ROBIN):** *Batman* Vol 1 #457 (Dec 1990) **SUBSIDIARY CATEGORY:** Genius Intelligence

36   St
Rb
Red Robin

Of all the Robins, Tim Drake is the outstanding detective. Even as a young boy he is incredibly perceptive, deducing the secret identities of Batman, Nightwing, and former Robin Jason Todd. He realizes that Batman needs a Robin to balance his darker side, and when Dick cannot be persuaded to become Robin again, Tim steps into the role. After Damian Wayne comes onto the scene, Tim becomes Red Robin to establish a new identity while still acknowledging his legacy. Tim possesses a genius intellect and is particularly adept when it comes to hacking computer systems. He is aware that, while he is an excellent fighter, he is not as skilled as the other Robins, so instead he makes sure he is the most prepared, with a plan for every eventuality.

RED HOOD

REAL NAME: Jason Todd **POWERS/ABILITIES:** Martial arts; weaponry skills **FIRST APPEARANCE (AS RED HOOD):** *Batman* Vol 1 #635 **SUBSIDIARY CATEGORY:** Metals

44   St
Hd
Red Hood

Jason Todd was the second Robin and the one with the most troubled path in life. A teenage car thief before being taken under Batman's wing, he is later killed by The Joker. Resurrected in a Lazarus Pit, he trains with the League of Assassins for a time before returning to Gotham City under the Red Hood moniker. His ruthless approach to fighting crime leads him to clash with Batman, but Jason believes that sometimes the only way to stop a violent criminal is to take them down with extreme prejudice. Eventually, he tries to put his more brutal instincts aside, no longer carrying firearms on missions and relying on the blunt force of his crowbar. But Jason will always face a struggle with his inner demons over how best to deal with severe and recurring threats like The Joker—should he show mercy, or take the worst bad guys off the board for good?

G.C.P.D.

REAL NAME: Various personnel **POWERS/ABILITIES:** Investigation; firearms training
FIRST APPEARANCE: *Detective Comics* Vol 1 #27 (May 1939)

Gotham City Police Department probably has the most challenging remits of any law-enforcement organization in the world. It patrols the streets of a city rife with a mix of criminals, including low-level chancers, warring gangland kingpins, and Gotham City's unique array of costumed felons.

For many years, the indefatigable head of the G.C.P.D. is Police Commissioner Jim Gordon, who rises to the top while trying to stamp out the corruption that had infested the department. Recognizing that Gotham City needs all the help it can get to make its streets safe, he builds a relationship with Batman, who others see as a dangerous vigilante. It is Gordon who places the Bat-Signal on the roof of G.C.P.D. HQ to summon Batman when he is needed and to send a warning to lawbreakers.

TOP BRASS

Although some G.C.P.D. officers are almost as immoral as the criminals, Gordon does surround himself with trustworthy colleagues. Renee Montoya supports him while he is standing in for Batman—she is reliable and brave, and committed to her vow to protect

and serve. She has trained under Harvey Bullock, a detective whose down-at-heel appearance and questionable methods do not stop Gordon from keeping him close as a key ally, and a G.C.P.D. detective who can be relied upon not to take bribes. It is Bullock who hires Maggie Sawyer, a good cop who becomes Commissioner for a time. Sawyer also has experience policing another Super-Villain hotspot, Metropolis, as does G.C.P.D. detective, Crispus Allen. Another sometime G.C.P.D. Commissioner is Jason Bard, although his tenure is dogged by controversy and it is eventually revealed that he has been compromised by the villain Hush.

Any police officer looking to face the ultimate test of their mettle and character will find it at the G.C.P.D.

When Batman temporarily steps down, Commissioner Gordon takes over, protected by a heavy Batsuit nicknamed "Rookie."

LOIS LANE

REAL NAME: Lois Lane **POWERS/ABILITIES:**
Investigative reporting **FIRST APPEARANCE:** *Action Comics* Vol 1 #1 (June 1938)

Lois Lane has spent her whole life fighting for truth and justice in her own way. As one of the world's leading investigative reporters—and a recipient of the Pulitzer Prize—she relentlessly pursues the corrupt and uplifts the downtrodden, bringing their stories into the sunlight of scrutiny. She has no metahuman powers, but she is taught basic fighting skills in her younger years by her military father. Lois is fiercely brave in the face of danger, and a formidable force against anyone who threatens her friends and family. She is married to Superman (Clark Kent), and their son Jon also shares the Superman moniker. Since the merging of two timelines resulting from the reality-warping activities of Mr. Mxyzptlk, Lois is the amalgam of two alternate Lois Lanes.

JIMMY OLSEN

REAL NAME: Jimmy Olsen **POWERS/ABILITIES:**
Photography; investigative reporting **FIRST APPEARANCE:** *Superman* Vol 1 #13 (Nov 1941)

Jimmy Olsen is a photojournalist and one of Clark Kent's best friends. He is a talented investigative reporter and, despite being born into wealth, is determined to make his mark in life on his own merits. Jimmy has no metahuman abilities, although sometimes being in the proximity of Superman means that he temporarily acquires bizarre powers. Like Lois Lane, Jimmy Olsen has won the Pulitzer Prize, in his case for a photo he took of Lex Luthor, and has also begun writing for the *Daily Planet* as well as taking pictures. Since Jimmy has a habit of getting into risky situations, he wears a Signal Watch that he can activate in an emergency to emit a hypersonic sound only audible to Superman.

IRIS WEST

REAL NAME: Iris West **POWERS/ABILITIES:**
Investigative reporting **FIRST APPEARANCE:** *Showcase* Vol 1 #4 (Oct 1956)

A determined and talented journalist, Iris West is also a pivotal member of The Flash Family. Aunt to The Flash (Wally West) and Kid Flash (Wallace West), Iris is also the wife and abiding love of the original Flash, Barry Allen. Barry describes her as the most fearless person he has ever known. Her adventurous life in pursuit of the stories that need to be told has enabled her to pick up a few useful skills along the way, like fixing engines and firing a gun. Iris is also an excellent undercover reporter, adept at disguising herself and blending into unfamiliar environments to get the information she is looking for. Whenever things do go south, Iris has gained enough combat tips from Barry and her nephews to defend herself if necessary.

LADY SHIVA

REAL NAME: Sandra Wu-San **POWERS/ABILITIES:** Elite martial artist, skilled in multiple fighting styles and with various weapons **FIRST APPEARANCE:** *Richard Dragon, Kung-Fu Fighter* Vol 1 #5 (Jan 1976)

Lady Shiva is one of the world's deadliest assassins, a master of martial arts almost without equal. She is highly adept in all known fighting disciplines, and even uses some "lost" combat styles from history. One such is Dim Mak, notable for its paralysis-causing blows. While she prefers the purity of fighting without weapons, she is skilled in using them, particularly traditional ones like katana swords and throwing stars. She is also an expert in reading body language, enabling her to predict her opponents' next moves. She teaches this valuable skill to her daughter, Cassandra Cain, who fights with the Batman Family as Orphan and then as one of the Batgirls. Shiva is the head of the League of Shadows, having become disillusioned with the direction of Rā's al Ghūl's League of Assassins and determined to set her own agenda.

CAPTAIN BOOMERANG

REAL NAME: George "Digger" Harkness **POWERS/ABILITIES:** Super-strength while in monstrous "dark radiation" form; skilled in making and throwing boomerangs **FIRST APPEARANCE:** *The Flash* Vol 1 #117 (Dec 1960) **SUBSIDIARY CATEGORY:** Energies: Nuclear/Radioactive

Originally from Australia, George "Digger" Harkness is highly skilled at both throwing and making boomerangs. He hopes to use this talent to get rich quick, traveling to Central City to become a thief with a difference. He has a flair for gadgetry, tweaking the designs of his boomerangs to give himself a range of "trick" weapons. These include explosive, electrified, and razor-sharp boomerangs. After a brush with dark radiation during Perpetua's attempted invasion of the Multiverse, Digger becomes a mutated, super-strong monster who throws boomerangs made from his own skeleton. After Perpetua's defeat, most of the side-effects of her actions on Earth disappear, but Captain Boomerang appears to retain the ability to transform. However, while in monstrous form he is so savage that he does not even recognize his former friends.

DEADSHOT

REAL NAME: Floyd Lawton **POWERS/ABILITIES:** Elite marksmanship; martial arts skills; mechanical engineering skills **FIRST APPEARANCE:** *Batman* Vol 1 #59 (Jun 1950)

Said—often by himself—to be the man who never misses, Floyd Lawton is the world's best marksman. He tells people that he grew up poor and taught himself to shoot after his parents and sister are accidentally killed by drug dealers, but this is a fiction. Floyd had rich but abusive parents, and he killed his beloved brother by mistake while trying to take down his violent father. After that, he vowed never to miss again. He becomes an assassin-for-hire, highly sought after thanks to his unmatched skills. For more specialized missions, Floyd, or Deadshot as he is better known, can design and create his own customized bullets. He also builds his own signature weapons, wrist-mounted machine guns, and a mask that both conceals his identity and aids in the precision of his aim.

ANCILLARY EXEMPLARS

There is an elite level of martial artists who can all claim to be among the world's best, largely operating in the shadows and by no means all on the side of justice. **Bronze Tiger** has been both hero and villain, and is a supremely skilled fighter as well as being able to tap into *qi* energy to speed his healing process. The assassin **Cheshire** is highly dangerous and has extensive knowledge of poisons, which she incorporates into her fighting by adding toxins to her weapons. Her daughter Lian (a.k.a. **Cheshire Cat**), conceived with the hero Arsenal (Roy Harper), is thought dead. However, Lian is actually under the radar as a Gotham City street kid, learning combat and survival skills. Another Arrow Family connection is the mercenary **Shado**, a superb archer and the mother of Red Arrow (Emiko Queen). Many heroes are taught martial arts by the great **Richard Dragon**, a peerless master of kung fu.

GREEN ARROW

REAL NAME: Oliver Queen **POWERS/ABILITIES:** World's finest archer; skilled martial artist
FIRST APPEARANCE: *More Fun Comics* Vol 1 #73 (Nov 1941)

8 St
Gr
Green Arrow

Born into privilege, Oliver Queen fritters his life away as a rich playboy until circumstances force him to change completely. Trapped on a deserted island, he learns survival skills and finally puts his old archery lessons—which his father forced him to take—to good use. Queen is so naturally talented with a bow and arrow that his ability verges on metahuman. He also realizes that he should be using his advantages to help others less fortunate, and from then on he becomes Green Arrow, trying to make a difference in whatever way he can. For the first time, he is earning something through his own hard work—his reputation as a hero.

Although generally favoring traditional arrows, Oliver's wealth means that he can devote extensive research and development resources to designing and building customized trick arrows. These have included explosive, adhesive, and even arrows tipped with boxing gloves.

PAYING IT FORWARD

Not all situations lend themselves to archery, so Green Arrow has also learned multiple martial arts to make himself a skilled hand-to-hand combatant, and an athlete in peak human condition. He has passed his knowledge on to his protégés in the Arrow Family, including first sidekick Roy Harper and half-sister Emiko. Kept grounded by his family and the love of his life, Black Canary, Oliver is a warrior for social justice, fighting to make life better for ordinary people. While he faces Multiversal threats as a member of the Justice League, Green Arrow never forgets about the "small" stuff—children going hungry on the streets of his city, or petty criminals ruining the lives of everyday folks.

Like the legendary Robin Hood, Green Arrow makes it his core mission principle to help the poor and oppressed.

ARSENAL

REAL NAME: Roy Harper **POWERS/ABILITIES:**
Elite-level archer; computer hacking; mechanical
engineering **FIRST APPEARANCE (AS ARSENAL):**
New Titans Vol 1 #99 (Jul 1993)

Roy Harper learned his incredible archery
skills from his adoptive father Big Bow,
a Native American of the Spokane tribe.
As a troubled teen runaway, Roy is taken
under the wing of Green Arrow (Oliver
Queen) and tries to get his life back on
track as a hero, known first as Speedy,
then Red Arrow, and eventually Arsenal.
His genius for engineering enables him
to design and build many trick arrows
to help him on missions, and he is also
a brilliant computer hacker. Roy is an
addict and has battled substance abuse
in his life, often with the help and support
of his many friends, both in the Arrow Family
and The Titans team, in which he finds
a second family.

RED ARROW

REAL NAME: Emiko Queen **POWERS/ABILITIES:**
Elite-level archer; martial artist; acrobat **FIRST
APPEARANCE:** *Green Arrow* Vol 5 #18 (May 2013)

Although she is Oliver Queen's half-sister—
they have the same father—Emiko is also
the daughter of the mercenary Shado, and
is raised to be an assassin by her adoptive
father, the villain Komodo (Simon Lacroix).

Rejecting this life, Emiko joins Green
Arrow as his apprentice, and the Emerald
Archer soon discovers that she is just
as gifted an archer as him. Her early
training has also made her an expert
hand-to-hand combatant and martial
artist. Training to be an assassin has given
Emiko a special talent in the art of stealth,
and she is an accomplished acrobat.
Feeling that she has earned the right
to call herself Green Arrow's partner rather
than his sidekick, Emiko takes the new
alias of Red Arrow.

GREEN ARROW

REAL NAME: Connor Hawke **POWERS/ABILITIES:**
Elite-level archer; martial artist **FIRST APPEARANCE:**
Green Arrow Vol 2 #0 (Oct 1994)

Connor Hawke is Oliver Queen's estranged
son, and takes over as Green Arrow when
his father is believed dead. As well as being
a proficient archer, Connor is also a master
martial artist, believed by Batman to be one
of the best hand-to-hand fighters in the
world. He learns archery from his father,
when Oliver ends up, by chance, at the
Buddhist monastery where Connor is then
living. Later, he joins the deadly League of
Shadows, where he is trained as an assassin,
perfecting the art of stealth and honing his
speed in combat. While he struggles with his
abandonment as a baby by his father, Connor
tries to use the Zen techniques he learned at
the monastery to reconcile his inner struggle
and build a relationship with the original
Green Arrow to forge a path forward.

AMANDA WALLER

REAL NAME: Amanda Waller **POWERS/ABILITIES:** Basic firearms and combat training; interrogation techniques **FIRST APPEARANCE:** *Legends* Vol 1 #1 (Nov 1986)

35   Ba
Wr
Amanda Waller

Amanda Waller is no metahuman, but her forceful personality is such that she has even very powerful beings living in fear of her. She is the ruthless government operative in charge of the Suicide Squad, the team of former villains who carry out dangerous black ops under threat of death. Nicknamed "The Wall," Amanda is motivated by the loss of her family to street criminals—she believes that conventional law enforcement is not working and tries to find a new way. Although she has basic firearms and combat training as a government agent, her real talents lie in interrogation and intimidation, with her iron will usually ensuring she gets her way, no matter who is opposing her. Having lost everything dear to her early in life, Amanda no longer has anything left to fear, making her both formidable and dangerous.

PEACEMAKER

REAL NAME: Chris Smith **POWERS/ABILITIES:** Martial arts and peak physical condition; firearms skills; helmet can emit blasts **FIRST APPEARANCE:** *Fightin' 5* Vol 1 #40 (Nov 1966) **SUBSIDIARY CATEGORY:** Amazing Armor and Wondrous Weapons

26   Vo
Pc
Peacemaker

Chris Smith is the personification of the old adage: "If you want peace, prepare for war." A former diplomat and special-forces soldier, he is so dedicated to the pursuit of peace that he is willing to do anything to achieve it—even kill. He wears a distinctive helmet which is bulletproof and can emit a sonic or laser blast to disorient opponents. After ending up in prison, he is recruited to be the new leader of the Suicide Squad. His helmet is given a further upgrade when it is lined to protect him from psionic attacks. He is at the peak of human physical condition, but mentally he is somewhat unstable due to an extremely troubled childhood. Chris has sometimes been known to talk to his helmet, and has at times believed that the spirits of those whom he has killed inhabit it and talk back to him.

STEVE TREVOR

REAL NAME: Steve Trevor **POWERS/ABILITIES:** Military training; espionage **FIRST APPEARANCE:** *All-Star Comics* Vol 1 #8 (Jan 1942)

While on a mission with the US Air Force, Steve Trevor is the only survivor of a plane crash. He is washed up on the shores of Themyscira, where he becomes the first human that Princess Diana meets. When she is chosen to accompany him back to the world of mortals, Steve becomes her ambassador and her guide in this strange new land. As a highly trained member of the military, Steve is at the peak of human physical condition and skilled in the use of firearms. He is an expert pilot. He also becomes adept in the art of espionage, working with some top-secret government organizations and later joining the shadowy Checkmate team.

JONAH HEX

REAL NAME: Jonah Hex **POWERS/ABILITIES:** Firearms skills; tracking abilities **FIRST APPEARANCE:** *All-Star Western* Vol 2 #10 (Mar 1972)

Jonah Hex is one of the best gunslingers in the Old West. Raised by Apache Native Americans from a young age after being sold to them by his father, he is never truly one of the Apache yet is also shunned by many white men. After being left for dead by his adopted brother Noh Tante, Jonah goes to fight on the Confederate side in the US Civil War, although he has some sympathies with the Union cause. On his return, he defeats Noh-Tante in a contest in which both men cheat—Jonah's punishment is exile from the tribe and having his face brutally scarred by a tomahawk. He becomes a feared mercenary for hire, selling his supreme quick-draw skills to the highest bidder.

ANCILLARY EXEMPLARS

The alias Manhunter is a legacy used by various vigilantes over the years. One such is **Paul Kirk**, a private detective with superlative hunting and tracking skills who becomes a costumed crime fighter after his friend is murdered. Many clones of Paul are later created to carry on his mission. **Mark Shaw** is a lawyer devoted to the legend of the ancient android Manhunters, who bypasses the law to bring down criminals himself. He later takes the alias of Leviathan to reshape the world. **Kate Spencer** is also an attorney—Green Arrow's, in fact—who balances the life of a vigilante with motherhood. **Rick Flag Jr.** is a military man who has lent his considerable skills to the more extreme crime fighting of the Suicide Squad.

THE ATOM

REAL NAME: Ryan Choi **POWERS/ABILITIES:** Size and density changing powered by Biobelt; prodigious intellect **FIRST APPEARANCE:** *Brave New World* Vol 1 #1 (Aug 2006) **SUBSIDIARY CATEGORY:** Genius Intelligence

Most people are only aware of the world directly around them, but there are levels of existence unseen by the human eye, including an incredible realm that is found only at the subatomic level. This is known as the Microverse, and it is the foundation of all reality—if it is damaged or even destroyed, the effect on the world above could be catastrophic. Quantum storms can be triggered, the lightning from which is a discharge of energy from tears in the membrane of reality itself, capable of rewriting time and space and obliterating memory and even truth. Although the Microverse is a physical place, it is also part of the nanostructure of Time, and in order to traverse it, an individual must not only be microscopically small but also able to cross the quantum barrier.

When The Atom (Ray Palmer) becomes trapped in the Microverse, grad student Ryan Choi takes on his heroic mantle to look for him. Ryan seems an unlikely hero as he

Down at subatomic size, The Atom can explore a whole new dimension of existence, containing its own beings, landscapes, and planets.

has multiple allergies, asthma, poor eyesight, and a nervous disposition. However, he has been providing research assistance and tech support for his professor, Ray Palmer, and becomes the first person that Ray trusts with the secret that he is also the size-changing Super Hero known as The Atom. Ryan is the only one of Ray's students who totally comprehends his class on kinematics—the geometry of motion. This study of a particle's trajectory can be applied to vast space phenomena as well as the smallest entities.

SHRINK MECHANICS

Ray has left Ryan a Biobelt, the device that he uses to change his size. The Biobelt has a core of material from a white dwarf star that enables the wearer to shrink to small sizes while maintaining base-level strength, which equates to proportional super-strength when shrunk. It can also be used to change the density of the body. The Biobelt works by moving a portion of the body's mass to or from an alternate dimension known as the Mass-Zone. To shrink in size, Ryan can send some of his mass to this dimension and bring it back when he is ready to return to normal size. He is the only person other than Ray Palmer to understand the Biobelt and how it works.

If Ryan needs to bring any Justice League or T-Council teammates to the Microverse, the Biobelt must be used in conjunction with a Shrinkship. Invented by Ray Palmer, this device uses gyroscopic controls and a white dwarf power source to transport multiple people to the Microverse, as long as they have been shrunk by the Biobelt first.

The Atom's real strength is his ability to see perspective and to appreciate the scale of the natural world. Even more so than his illustrious predecessor, Ryan Choi is able to use that ability in an empathic way to understand the points of view of everyone whom he tries to help. He knows that small things matter, and that sometimes they can have the most significant impact.

THE ATOM

REAL NAME: Ray Palmer **POWERS/ABILITIES:** Size and density changing powered by Biobelt; prodigious intellect **FIRST APPEARANCE:** *Showcase* Vol 1 #34 (Oct 1961) **SUBSIDIARY CATEGORY:** Genius Intelligence

Ray Palmer is a brilliant scientist who loves solving problems, particularly other people's. He is a professor of physics at a prestigious college. Ray sees science as a world of imagination in which anything can be achieved with the right application of hard work and intellect, and as a consequence he is an exceptional inventor. His most incredible creation is the Biobelt, incorporating a white dwarf star lens into the buckle that enables him to shrink down to sizes too small to be seen by the human eye.

Ray maintains his usual strength while at miniature sizes, making him proportionally super-strong. He can also change the mass of individual parts of his body—to generate a super-strong punch, for example. He can also adjust his density, allowing him to phase through solid objects or become ultra-dense to protect himself against attack.

SMALL WORLD

His work in this niche also leads Ray to discover the Microverse, a plane of existence beneath our own that is at once tiny and vast. After Ryan Choi also takes on the mantle of The Atom, Ray decides to base himself in the Microverse, taking the opportunity to study it further but also protecting it from threats. Ray further discovers that in the Microverse, where everything is tiny, he can use the Biobelt to make himself a relative giant.

Ray's perspective on reality is almost unique, and this, coupled with his ingenious scientific mind, makes him an invaluable ally and friend to other Super Heroes. His work is constantly pushing at the boundaries of the possible.

While best-known for his shrinking ability, in the Microverse Ray Palmer can grow to relatively giant sizes.

BLUE BEETLE

REAL NAME: Jaime Reyes **POWERS/ABILITIES:** Connection to alien scarab bestows armor, a range of weapons, and flight **FIRST APPEARANCE (AS BLUE BEETLE):** *Infinite Crisis* Vol 1 #5 (Apr 2006) **SUBSIDIARY CATEGORY:** Alien Origins, Magical

Jaime Reyes is still in high school when he comes across a blue scarab, a beetle-shaped artifact that immediately connects with him, embedding itself into his spine. The scarab gives Jaime a wide range of powers, turning into a protective, carapacelike armor, deploying wings for flight, and shape-shifting to form a variety of weapons. However, the scarab is not merely an object, as Jaime soon realizes when it starts communicating with him as a voice in his head, and even controlling his actions when it feels it necessary. The scarab is a piece of alien technology built by the Reach, and having come to Earth thousands of years previously, it also acquires magical properties in Ancient Egypt. Jaime forms a symbiotic relationship with the scarab, which enables him to be the most powerful Blue Beetle there has ever been.

BLUE BEETLE

REAL NAME: Ted Kord **POWERS/ABILITIES:** Martial arts skills; prodigious intellect **FIRST APPEARANCE:** *Captain Atom* Vol 1 #83 (Nov 1966) **SUBSIDIARY CATEGORY:** Genius Intelligence

Ted Kord wants to use the wealth he inherits from his father to make a difference, to invent technological solutions to improve people's lives. He is also a great admirer of Super Heroes, and builds himself a protective, gadget-packed suit so that he can emulate them. All he lacks is a name, until he runs into neighbor Dan Garrett, an archaeologist who shows him a mysterious insect-shaped artifact. As Blue Beetle, Ted brings his phenomenal intellect and creativity to the world of crime fighting, as well as an impressive range of martial arts skills. Among the technological aids he designs and builds is a vehicle known as the Bug, predominantly an aircraft but also with diving capabilities. Inside it is a mobile crime lab so that Ted can conduct investigations in the field. When heart problems force him to step back from active adventuring, Ted becomes mentor and support to the new Blue Beetle (Jaime Reyes).

STEEL

REAL NAME: John Henry Irons **POWERS/ABILITIES:** Power Armor gives super-strength, durability, and flight; wields kinetic hammer; prodigious intellect **FIRST APPEARANCE:** *Adventures of Superman* Vol 1 #500 (Jun 1993) **SUBSIDIARY CATEGORY:** Genius Intelligence

John Henry Irons is an engineering genius who uses his knowledge of mechanics to build an armored suit. Inspired by Superman, he too wants to protect the people of Metropolis and the wider world from harm, and wears an "S" symbol and cape as a tribute to Kal-El. As the hero Steel, John Henry's suit offers him the ability to fly via jet boots, and gives him super-strength and durability. To manifest the Power Armor on his body, John Henry needs only to tap his chest. As well as his armor, John Henry also carries his signature weapon, the kinetic hammer. The hammer gathers kinetic energy as it moves through the air, so the farther it is thrown, the more powerful a blow it strikes when it hits its target. It also has electromagnetic capabilities, and can be controlled by John Henry's voice, including returning to him on command.

STEEL

REAL NAME: Natasha Irons **POWERS/ABILITIES:** Power Armor gives super-strength, durability, and flight; wields kinetic hammer; genius intellect **FIRST APPEARANCE (AS STEEL):** *Action Comics* Vol 1 #806 (Oct 2003) **SUBSIDIARY CATEGORY:** Genius Intelligence

Natasha Irons is the niece of John Henry Irons, and is largely brought up by him in Metropolis. Like him, she is a technological genius, and as soon as she can she is helping him build and maintain his armor and weapons. This know-how enables her to build her own steel suit, which, like her uncle's, offers super-strength, durability, and jet-powered flight. However, Natasha's more advanced suit can be put on and taken off by a mental command. Natasha also deploys a kinetic hammer as her weapon. She prefers semisentient chrome, which can compress objects to a tiny "quantum package" for easy transportation and be returned to full size when needed with a blow of Natasha's hammer. She joins The Titans, building them the Boom Room, a vehicle for near-instant transport anywhere in the world.

STARMAN

REAL NAME: Jack Knight **POWERS/ABILITIES:** Cosmic Staff gives flight, force fields, stellar energy blasts, and levitation **FIRST APPEARANCE:** *Zero Hour: Crisis in Time* Vol 1 #1 (Sep 1994)

Jack Knight inherits the title of Starman in tragic circumstances. His father Ted, the original Starman, has retired and passed the name on to his eldest son David. When David is killed by one of Ted's old enemies, Jack reluctantly agrees to take over, although he refuses to wear the brightly colored costume. He would almost pass for a regular guy, if it weren't for the fact that he wields the incredibly potent Cosmic Staff. Built by Jack's father, a gifted scientist, the staff absorbs the energy of stars, which can be fired out as powerful blasts or distributed around the user as a force field. It can also enable flight, or levitate other objects. The Cosmic Staff is designed to be so attuned to its owner that it responds to their mental commands.

STARGIRL

REAL NAME: Courtney Whitmore **POWERS/ABILITIES:** Belt gives enhanced strength, speed, stamina, durability, and reflexes; Cosmic Staff gives flight, force fields, stellar energy blasts, and levitation
FIRST APPEARANCE: *Stars and S.T.R.I.P.E.* Vol 1 #0 (Jul 1999)

Courtney Whitmore is a legacy hero in more ways than one. Not only does she inherit the Cosmic Staff—which she nicknames "Cosmo"—from Starman, her stepfather Pat Dugan also has a heroic past as Stripesy, sidekick to the Star-Spangled Kid and the inspiration for Courtney's Super Hero identity. She also wears a belt of his making that adapts the technology of the Cosmic Staff to bestow its wielder with enhanced strength, speed, stamina, durability, and reflexes, and the ability to fire out "shooting stars." So it is not surprising that Courtney is extremely knowledgeable about the history of costumed heroes. Although she is a regular, fun-loving teenage girl, Courtney throws herself into the life of a Super Hero, trying to fit it in around her schoolwork. When he can, Pat dons an armored suit and acts as her protective sidekick S.T.R.I.P.E.

BOOSTER GOLD

REAL NAME: Michael Jon Carter **POWERS/ABILITIES:** Time travel using Time Sphere;
Power Suit provides super-strength and durability; Legion Flight Ring enables flight
FIRST APPEARANCE: *Booster Gold* Vol 1 #1 (Feb 1986)

34   St
Bo
Booster Gold

Booster Gold is Michael Jon Carter, a man out of time. He is a former sportsman from the 25th century, disgraced after a gambling scandal he took part in to pay his mother's medical bills. Stealing a Time Sphere and a costume from a Super Hero museum, he travels back to the 21st century in order to become famous as a hero himself. Eventually Michael adopts a new, more serious attitude toward being a hero, and takes the role of a protector of the timestream. He knows the most important part of traveling through time is the need to be in and out before creating any unwanted effects. He is always accompanied by Skeets, a flying robotic assistant who provides advice and information. Booster Gold can also fly, thanks to a Legion Flight Ring, and his purloined Power Suit provides super-strength and durability.

ADAM STRANGE

REAL NAME: Adam Strange **POWERS/ABILITIES:** Rannian technology provides jet pack for flight and a laser gun **FIRST APPEARANCE:** *Showcase* Vol 1 #17 (Dec 1958) **SUBSIDIARY CATEGORY:** Alien Origins

19   St
Ag
Adam Strange

Although he himself is a regular human from Earth, archaeologist Adam Strange is the chosen champion of the planet Rann. He travels back and forth between his homeworld and his adopted world via Zeta-Beams, a technology developed by Rannian scientist Sardath. Originally intended for communication purposes only, the Zeta-Beams became infused with radiation and develop into a teleportation system. On Rann, Adam is equipped with a costume, a jet pack for flight, and a laser gun so that he can help its people face threats to their safety, usually from warlike rival planets. But when the radiation from the Zeta-Beam wears off, he is instantly transported back to Earth. The time and place that the next Zeta-Beam will hit Earth can be predicted, so Adam tries to ensure he can return to Rann whenever he can. This is especially important as he marries a Rannian woman, Sardath's daughter Alanna.

SANDMAN

REAL NAME: Wesley Dodds **POWERS/ABILITIES:** Prophetic dreams; Gas Gun fires sleeping gas; skilled hand-to-hand fighter **FIRST APPEARANCE:** *Adventure Comics* Vol 1 #40 (Jul 1939) **SUBSIDIARY CATEGORY:** Sphere of the Gods, Genius Intelligence

Wesley Dodds is chosen by the entity Dream to have prophetic visions while he sleeps. Although these can be cryptic, Wesley has a brilliant investigative mind and can usually interpret them. This enables him to have a unique insight into future events and any potential threats or crimes that may happen, so he becomes the adventurer Sandman. His signature weapon is his Gas Gun, which releases sleeping gas to incapacitate all in the vicinity. So that he is not affected by it, Wesley incorporates a gas mask into his costume. He also carries a "wirepoon" gun for easy navigation of city blocks—it fires a length of steel cable that can be used either for climbing walls or swinging between buildings.

GUARDIAN

REAL NAME: Jim Harper **POWERS/ABILITIES:** Shield gives protection and hovers in air; hand-to-hand fighting skills; peak physical condition **FIRST APPEARANCE:** *Star-Spangled Comics* Vol 1 #7 (Apr 1942)

Jim Harper is a Metropolis-based police officer who becomes a vigilante in the years following the Great Depression, protecting citizens under the codename Guardian. Although he has no metahuman powers, he uses a distinctive golden shield for both protection and transport, because it uses antigravity capabilities to hover and move through the air. It is also said to be indestructible. Jim is highly athletic and a good hand-to-hand fighter. He is aided by the Newsboy Legion, a group of tearaway children whom Jim wants to stay out of reform school by keeping them occupied. When the Newsboy Legion grow up, they become scientists and get involved in a project to clone their old mentor, Guardian.

KATANA

REAL NAME: Tatsu Yamashiro **POWERS/ABILITIES:** Martial arts **FIRST APPEARANCE:** *The Brave and the Bold* Vol 1 #200 (Jul 1983) **SUBSIDIARY CATEGORY:** Magical

Katana is a highly skilled fighter with a tragic past. When her family is killed by her maniacal brother-in-law, wielding a magical, centuries-old sword known as Soultaker, Katana—Tatsu as she was known then— fights him, and the sword chooses her as its new owner. The blade contains the souls of some of the people whom it has killed, and Katana occasionally hears their voices speaking to her. Due to its magical properties, it is even effective against Kryptonians. With her family gone, Katana devotes her life to tracking down gangsters who cause misery to other families and taking revenge on them. She is an elite martial artist, and an expert fighter with her blade.

CAPTAIN COLD

REAL NAME: Leonard Snart **POWERS/ABILITIES:** Effects of metahuman upgrade give cryokinesis; cold gun slows molecules of targets to absolute zero **FIRST APPEARANCE:** *Showcase* Vol 1 #8 (Jun 1957) **SUBSIDIARY CATEGORY:** Lab Created

Leonard Snart is Captain Cold, leader of the Rogues. At the start of his career he is armed only with his cold gun, a weapon designed and built by himself that slows down the movement of its targets by cooling the atoms within them to absolute zero. This is particularly effective against speedsters like his regular nemesis The Flash. Later, Len is able to upgrade to meta-human powers, first when a scientist gives him the chance to fuse his DNA with his cold gun, and secondly when Lex Luthor offers power boosts to a number of villains in exchange for their support of his war on Justice. After this, Captain Cold's absolute zero technology becomes a part of him, giving him the ability to cool the air around him to create weather systems and freeze people and objects.

BLACK MANTA

REAL NAME: David Hyde **POWERS/ABILITIES:** Suit gives protection against ocean environment and fast swimming; mask provides enhanced vision and fires optic blasts; prodigious intellect; hand-to-hand combat skills **FIRST APPEARANCE:** *Aquaman* Vol 1 #35 (Aug 1967) **SUBSIDIARY CATEGORY:** Genius intelligence

David Hyde has a long-running and bitter feud with Aquaman (Arthur Curry). While David has distant ancestors from Atlantis, he is more or less a regular human, so he must use a wide range of technological enhancements to become Black Manta. This allows him to go toe to toe with the powerful Atlantean. David is a genius engineer, and designs a suit and mask to enable him to survive the harsh ocean environment. He can travel to great depths without suffering from the increased pressure or decreased oxygen and temperature levels. The suit incorporates a propulsion system so that Black Manta can move rapidly underwater. His distinctive black mask has red lenses over his eyes that give enhanced vision even in the murky depths; they also fire out energy blasts in combat situations.

JERVIS TETCH

REAL NAME: Jervis Tetch **POWERS/ABILITIES:** Can control the minds of others using technology he created; prodigious intellect **FIRST APPEARANCE:** *Batman* Vol 1 #49 (Oct 1948) **SUBSIDIARY CATEGORY:** Genius intelligence

15	Vo
Ha	
Jervis Tetch	

Since childhood Jervis Tetch has had a hormone deficiency that prevents him from growing. His attempts to medicate the condition leave him addicted to drugs and mentally unstable. His fixation on a girl at his school named Alice leads him to become obsessed with the tale of *Alice in Wonderland*, and he styles himself The Mad Hatter in homage to that story. The signature weapon in his crimes is a mind-control device, usually embedded in the brim of a hat worn by himself or by others who have been tricked or persuaded. With these, Jervis can induce others to do his bidding, trigger certain emotions, and also block similar attacks on himself. Although criminally insane, Jervis is also a genius with a great understanding of the workings of the human mind.

BLACK MASK

REAL NAME: Roman Sionis **POWERS/ABILITIES:** Skilled with firearms; intimidation tactics **FIRST APPEARANCE:** *Batman* Vol 1 #386 (Aug 1985)

33	Tx
Fs	
Black Mask	

Roman Sionis is a formerly legitimate businessman who ends up in the more sinister business of organized crime. Although he inherits a fortune after killing his parents, he runs his cosmetics empire into the ground with a series of poor business decisions, and decides he is more suited to life in Gotham City's seedy underworld. He wears a mask carved from the ebony wood of his parents' coffins, both to intimidate opponents and to cover the scarring on his face. He runs his criminal empire with ruthless brutality, commanding an army of gangsters who loyally carry out his orders. Roman's sanity has been called into question, particularly when it comes to his mask— it is possible that he sees it as a separate personality, enabling him to blame his more violent crimes on the Black Mask rather than on himself.

LEX LUTHOR

6   Vo

Lx

Lex Luthor

REAL NAME: Lex Luthor **POWERS/ABILITIES:** Genius intellect
FIRST APPEARANCE: *Action Comics* Vol 1 #23 (Apr 1940)
SUBSIDIARY CATEGORY: Amazing Armor and Wondrous Weapons

Metahuman powers might seem like the ultimate tool for a person to achieve everything they ever dreamed of, but there are a select few who attempt to realize their most ambitious goals using only their human attributes. Lex Luthor is the best example of this that Earth has to offer. Some Super-Villains have formidable powers or terrifying appearances, but Lex has become one of the world's most dangerous individuals while usually wearing a tailored business suit and possessing no metahuman abilities at all—merely the power of his brilliant mind.

Despite being a billionaire businessman thanks to successfully running LexCorp, Lex wants more. When the alien Superman appears on Earth with his incredible powers, Lex's ego cannot handle the idea that there may be a being superior to him. Framing his narcissism as suspicion of the alien's motives and viewing himself almost as a champion of humankind, Lex sets out to prove his worth by defeating the Man of Steel.

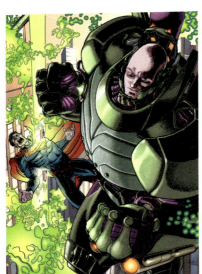

While businesspeople in power suits is nothing new, Lex Luthor takes it to a new level, building a mech armor that incorporates Kryptonite to even the odds against his Kryptonian nemesis.

He applies his genius intellect and talent for invention and engineering to design a battlesuit that would enable someone of merely human physiology to take on a Kryptonian powered by Earth's yellow sun. Lex's armored suit gives him extreme durability and super-strength, but even this would not be enough to damage Superman at his full strength. Knowing this, Lex integrates Kryptonite into the suitto weaken his opponent and

therefore make him more vulnerable to the armor's offensive weaponry. Since Superman can fly, Lex has to as well, fitting rocket boosters to the underside of the armor's feet. The suit's gauntlets have the capability of firing powerful energy blasts, and the whole costume is protected by a force field. Lex has had many such suits, as he is always looking to improve on his design to get the edge over his opponents. Despite his scorn for aliens in general, he is happy to adapt their technology to his own advantage, including using an Apokolyptian Mother Box to enable teleportation.

APEX LEX

Lex is not always without metahuman powers. When he allies with the phenomenally powerful Perpetua, she rewards him with godlike abilities. He is given a hybrid human/Martian body, but with powers exceeding that of either species, including reality-hopping travel and the capability of wielding any of the creative energies of the Multiverse. Lex decides to use his near-omnipotence to empower others, offering members of his Legion of Doom upgraded tech or metahuman powers in exchange for their loyalty. However, Luthor is returned to his human form when he displeases Perpetua. Characteristically, he tells her that he never needed metahuman powers anyway.

While the Justice League rightfully mistrusts Lex Luthor and regards him as one of their most dangerous opponents, despite their apparent power mismatch, he is not always a force for evil on Earth. He has even saved the planet before, and allied with Super Heroes against external threats, but the fact remains that nothing is more important to Lex Luthor than Lex Luthor.

THE PENGUIN

REAL NAME: Oswald Cobblepot **POWERS/ABILITIES:** Prodigious intellect **FIRST APPEARANCE:** *Detective Comics* Vol 1 #58 (Dec 1941) **SUBSIDIARY CATEGORY:** Transformative Science

Oswald Cobblepot's odd appearance might have made him a figure of fun at one time, but the wily bird has worked his way up to the top of the pile in Gotham City's overpopulated organized crime circles. As The Penguin, Oswald uses his considerable intellect to outwit rivals and evade capture by law enforcement. He rules the roost from his personal nightclub, the Iceberg Lounge, waiting for his innumerable contacts to bring him intel from all over Gotham City and beyond.

GENTLEMAN OF CRIME

The Penguin considers himself a cut above the rest of the city's hoodlums and costumed villains. He is always dapper, often sporting a top hat and monocle, and carries a variety of umbrellas. These are not just to complete his look, however, but often conceal deadly surprises like poison gas or a machine-gun. Although he may present the outward appearance of an eccentric gentleman, The Penguin should not be underestimated. He is ruthless and deadly, stopping at nothing to consolidate his power or take revenge for a perceived

slight. He has learned early in life that it doesn't matter whether people are good or bad, only what they can do for you, and this philosophy inevitably brings him into conflict with Batman. The Penguin also believes that he, Oswald Cobblepot, not the Dark Knight, truly controls crime in Gotham City. He is the one pulling all the strings behind the scenes, with money and weapons distributed to other villains according to his whim. So only he, not Batman or any other law enforcer, can bring down the crime rate.

The Penguin was born with his beaklike nose and small stature, but he learns to ignore the taunts and make the most of his intelligence to beat the bullies—and everyone else.

THE SCARECROW

7   Tx
Sr
The Scarecrow

REAL NAME: Jonathan Crane **POWERS/ABILITIES:**
Able to induce hallucinations of someone's worst fears
using Fear Toxin; prodigious intellect; toxicology **FIRST
APPEARANCE:** *World's Finest* Vol 1 #3 (Sep 1941)

The emotion of fear is Jonathan Crane's
constant childhood companion, and he grows
up to be mentally unstable and obsessed with
terror. He is a brilliant scientist, especially in the
fields of psychology and toxicology. He is
familiar with every known phobia, and takes
great delight in inducing fear in others. He does
this not only with his unsettling Scarecrow
costume, but also with his Fear Toxin. This
concoction is designed to cause hallucinations
that manifest the victim's greatest fear, and is
capable of affecting even extremely powerful
beings. The Scarecrow's own greatest fear is
Batman himself. For his part, the Dark Knight
has learned from bitter experience to carry
an antidote to Scarecrow's Fear Toxin.

THE RIDDLER

14   Vo
Ri
The Riddler

REAL NAME: Edward Nigma **POWERS/ABILITIES:**
Mechanical engineering; prodigious intellect **FIRST
APPEARANCE:** *Detective Comics* Vol 1 #140 (Oct 1948)

While Edward Nigma is a genius, adept
at devising and building intricate traps
and weapons, he also has a significant
psychological flaw that causes his schemes
ultimately to fail. His need for attention is such
that he cannot help leaving riddles at his crime
scenes—which plays right into the hands
of Batman, the World's Greatest Detective.
Although The Riddler's brain could be said
to be his main weapon, he also carries
a staff topped by a question mark, which he
sometimes rigs to deliver electric shocks or
act as a remote control for his devilish devices.
The Riddler spends a good deal of time
incarcerated at Arkham Asylum, although
he claims that he can escape whenever he
chooses, thanks to his analytical genius.

ANCILLARY EXEMPLARS

64   Vo
Tc
Trickster

51   Vo
Hs
Hugo Strange

67   Vo
Py
Professor Pyg

The villain community is richly populated
with geniuses who have decided to devote
their intellect to building dangerous devices
or creating deadly monsters. One villain fond
of pranks and gadgets is the **Trickster**,
sometime member of the Rogues. While
he uses a wide range of devices, his best
invention is perhaps his antigravity boots,
which allow him to levitate and move around
in the air. **Hugo Strange** is a psychologist
who uses his genius for evil, and creates
Monster Men, corpses revived with a serum
mutating them into undead horrors to cause
havoc. Pig-mask-wearing **Professor Pyg**
also creates monstrosities, although he
believes they are necessary steps on the
road to perfection. His Dollotrons are living
humans transformed by surgery into "dolls."

MISTER TERRIFIC

REAL NAME: Michael Holt **POWERS/ABILITIES:** T-Spheres provide weapons array and flight; martial arts; peak athleticism; prodigious intellect **FIRST APPEARANCE:** *Spectre* Vol 3 #54 (Jun 1997) **SUBSIDIARY CATEGORY:** Amazing Armor and Wondrous Weapons

41   St
Mt
Mister Terrific

Michael Holt is a human phenomenon who certainly merits the title of Mister Terrific. He is the perfect example of a polymath, with a natural ability to learn new skills and acquire knowledge. He is an Olympic champion in the decathlon and a billionaire CEO of a company he founded himself. Aiding him in every aspect of life are his T-Spheres, hovering spherical devices that have a wide range of uses. They can impart information either through sound or image projection; be used as explosive or projectile weapons; and support Michael's weight, enabling him to fly. Always hovering nearby, the T-Spheres support Mister Terrific in his lifelong quest for learning, constantly teaching and testing him. His diverse knowledge and genius intelligence make him a natural investigator as well as a respected Super Hero.

RIP HUNTER

REAL NAME: Unknown **POWERS/ABILITIES:** Prodigious intellect, builds Time Sphere to travel anywhere in the timestream **FIRST APPEARANCE:** *Showcase* Vol 1 #20 (Jun 1959)

20   St
Rp
Rip Hunter

Rip Hunter is a gifted scientist from the future who has mastered the technology required for time travel. He is known as the Time Master, and is the leader of a group of time-travelers who watch over the timestream. His activities are so potentially dangerous that he operates as secretively as he can. Knowing that this would be his future, his parents raised him with care, protecting him from potential time-hopping threats. He has never revealed his real name to anyone, and uses "Rip Hunter" as an alias to cover up his true past and protect those connected to him. His biggest secret is that his real father is the hero Booster Gold, and, like Booster, Rip uses a Time Sphere to travel through the timestream. This presents the curious, paradoxical scenario in which Rip designs and builds a Time Sphere that his own father uses before he does.

WILL MAGNUS

23	St
Wi	
Will Magnus	

REAL NAME: Will Magnus **POWERS/ABILITIES:** Prodigious intellect, expert in robotics and metallurgy **FIRST APPEARANCE:** *Showcase* Vol 1 #37 (Apr 1962)

Will Magnus is a brilliant but erratic scientist who specializes in robotics, and is the creator of the Metal Men. Will designs and builds the Responsometer, a device that animates molten metal into a humanoid shape and gives it its personality and characteristics taken from the materia in which the Responsometer is submerged. Despite his success, Will struggles to find his place in the scientific community, resenting the attention given to people he believes are less accomplished than he is. He has won awards for his apparently groundbreaking Metal Men, but Will feels guilt and impostor syndrome over this, as, in reality, the Responsometers merely contain echoes of his own personality, not true independent life.

NILES CAULDER

24	St
Nc	
Niles Caulder	

REAL NAME: Niles Caulder **POWERS/ABILITIES:** Prodigious intellect, surgeon **FIRST APPEARANCE:** *My Greatest Adventure* Vol 1 #80 (Jun 1963)

Niles Caulder is the founder and Chief of the Doom Patrol, and an outstanding scientist. However, he operates on an "end justifies the means" basis, committing various unscrupulous acts in pursuit of what he deems the greater good. He engineers accidents for several of the original members of the Doom Patrol, giving them bizarre abilities without their knowledge or consent. An egregious example of this attitude is Niles' use of his skills to successfully implant the human brain of racecar driver Cliff Steele into an android body to create Robotman. His reckless experimentation on their bodies eventually alienates the Doom Patrol from Niles, and they fire him as leader.

ANCILLARY EXEMPLARS

59	St
Lb	
Silas Stone	

55	Vo
Mw	
T. O. Morrow	

54	Vo
Pi	
Professor Ivo	

65	Vo
Vc	
Veronica Cale	

Silas Stone is a top scientist at S.T.A.R. Labs who uses his extensive knowledge to rebuild his son Victor's body after a terrible injury, making him Cyborg. Professor **T. O. Morrow** also works at S.T.A.R. Labs, specializing in robotics, and is the creator of the Red Tornado and Tomorrow Woman. When the Dark Multiverse invasion is imminent, Morrow teams up with other scientific mavericks to stop the forces of Barbatos. Alongside him is old colleague **Professor Ivo,** creator of the Amazo robot, and **Veronica Cale**, the tech entrepreneur who is also an enemy of Wonder Woman.

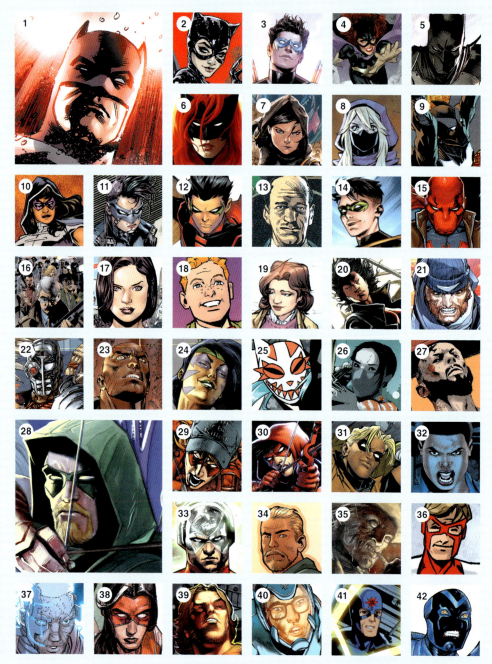

ALIEN ORIGINS

Earth is not alone … The Multiverse is home to many inhabited planets and a vast range of fascinating alien species, some of whom come in peace, and others to conquer.

KRYPTONIAN

There remains in existence survivors from the destroyed planet of Krypton, renowned for their prodigious powers in certain star systems.

MARTIANS

Closer to home are the native inhabitants of Mars, now largely wiped out, although the survivors possess remarkable abilities.

EXTRAORDINARY EXTRATERRESTRIALS

Many powerful individuals from other planets have come into contact with Earth, however, the friendliness of these encounters varies greatly.

6 Ba **Le** Legion of Super-Heroes	**18** St **Sf** Starfire	**21** St **Tw** Wonder Twins	**24** St **Ph** Phantom Girl	**7** Vo **Br** Brainiac	**14** Ba **Bv** Brainiac 5	**37** Vo **Ch** Shade, the Changing Man
41 St **Sh** Shade, the Changing Girl	**34** Vo **Ul** Ultra the Multi-Alien	**20** Vo **Lo** Lobo	**10** Tx **St** Starro	**19** Vo **Mg** Mongul	**11** Co **De** Despero	**3** Vo **Mi** Mister Mind
38 St **Js** Jemm, Son of Saturn	**29** Vo **Kj** Kanjar Ro	**30** Vo **Jx** Jax-Ur	**39** Vo **Lz** Lor-Zod	**33** Vo **Qb** Queen Bee		

ALIEN CIVILIZATIONS

Just like Earth, each inhabited world has its own unique history and customs, forming a culture that shapes its entire population.

2 St **Kp** Kryptonians	**12** Vo **Th** Thanagarians	**8** St **Rn** Rannians	**16** St **Dx** Daxamites	**36** Vo **Dm** Dominators	**40** Vo **Re** The Reach	**28** Vo **Du** Durlans
31 Vo **Ax** Appellaxians	**32** Vo **Gi** Gil'Dishpan	**35** Vo **Kh** Khund				

SUPERMAN

REAL NAME: Kal-El/Clark Kent **POWERS:** Super-strength, speed, durability, stamina, reflexes; heightened senses; flight; heat vision; freeze breath **FIRST APPEARANCE:** *Action Comics* Vol 1 #1 (Jun 1938) **SUBSIDIARY CATEGORY:** Energies: Light

Superman is one of the most powerful individuals in the universe, but his exceptionality could be said to be almost happenstance. What makes him so remarkable is not a rare metagene, but his own natural biology, and the course of events that brought him to Earth as one of the very few survivors of his home planet. Superman, or Kal-El to use his original name, would have been a regular Kryptonian had he grown up and lived a normal life on Krypton instead of being ejected from the dying home planet as a baby. He would also have no superpowers if his escape craft had not found its way to a life-supporting planet in the solar system of a yellow star.

On Earth, the planet Kal-El now calls home, he is an extraordinary being. Raised as Clark Kent in rural Kansas, as he grows to adulthood, he soon discovers he has a dizzying array of superpowers, and these all stem from where he now finds himself located in space. Krypton, his homeworld, was a massive planet with extremely strong gravitational forces. Kryptonians evolved to have a dense molecular structure to withstand these forces and thrive;

One of Superman's most potent abilities is the "solar flare," when he expels all the solar energy stored in his cells in one single, powerful blast.

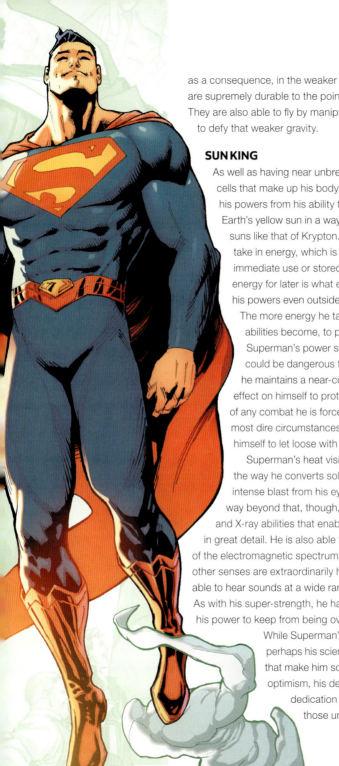

as a consequence, in the weaker gravity of Earth, Kryptonians are supremely durable to the point of total invulnerability. They are also able to fly by manipulating graviton particles to defy that weaker gravity.

SUN KING

As well as having near unbreakable bonds between the cells that make up his body, Superman gets the bulk of his powers from his ability to metabolize radiation from Earth's yellow sun in a way that is impossible under red suns like that of Krypton. Solar receptors in his skin take in energy, which is then either converted for immediate use or stored. This ability to hold excess energy for later is what enables Superman to retain his powers even outside of Earth's solar system.

The more energy he takes in, the stronger his abilities become, to phenomenal levels. In fact, Superman's power set is so formidable that he could be dangerous to Earth. To counteract this, he maintains a near-constant mental dampening effect on himself to protect the innocent in the vicinity of any combat he is forced to enter into. Only in the most dire circumstances does the Man of Steel allow himself to let loose with his full strength.

Superman's heat vision is a very visible example of the way he converts solar energy, in this case as an intense blast from his eyes. His vision powers extend way beyond that, though, to microscopic, telescopic, and X-ray abilities that enable him to examine things in great detail. He is also able to perceive different parts of the electromagnetic spectrum. Additionally, Superman's other senses are extraordinarily heightened, including being able to hear sounds at a wide range of volumes and pitches. As with his super-strength, he has to mentally focus to control his power to keep from being overwhelmed.

While Superman's powers inspire awe, it is perhaps his scientifically unmeasurable qualities that make him so special: his unwavering optimism, his devotion to justice, and his dedication to using his gifts to protect those unable to protect themselves.

SUPERGIRL

REAL NAME: Kara Zor-El **POWERS:** Super-strength, speed, durability, stamina; heightened senses; flight; heat vision; freeze breath; sonic scream **FIRST APPEARANCE:** *Action Comics* #252 (May 1959) **SUBSIDIARY CATEGORY:** Energies: Light

Supergirl, unlike many of Earth's heroes, does not possess a metagene giving her powers, but instead acquires them from the way in which her alien DNA reacts to the Sun's energy.

As a teenager, Kara Zor-El was one of the only survivors of the destruction of the planet Krypton, sent away by her father in a rocket that took her eventually to Earth, where she was reunited with her cousin Kal-El (Superman). Like him, Kara had powers that were fueled by the yellow sun of the Solar System, and she consequently became Supergirl, one of the most formidable heroes on the planet.

SOLAR BATTERY

Kara is able to absorb energy from the Sun, which then undergoes a process in her body to convert it into the incredible abilities that she exhibits, like flight, X-ray or heat vision, and super-strength, among many others. It is not just Earth's star that affects Supergirl; any yellow sun has the same effect. In the vast universe, stars of other colors can be found: red suns, such as the one which used to warm Krypton, can take away her powers, while green suns not only render her powerless but also cause excruciating pain. Blue suns emit more energy than yellow ones, and as such can increase Supergirl's powers and possibly even add new ones, but exposure carries a risk of overloading.

In addition to certain colored stars, Kara's powers can be adversely affected by magic and Kryptonite. It is also thought that the continual need to restrain her powers, to prevent a loss of control leading to potential harm for bystanders, causes Supergirl a lot of effort and even pain, although she herself has not acknowledged this.

JON KENT, SUPERMAN

REAL NAME: Jonathan Kent **POWERS:** Super-strength, speed, durability, stamina; heightened senses; flight; heat vision; freeze breath **FIRST APPEARANCE:** *Convergence: Superman* #2 (Jul 2015) **SUBSIDIARY CATEGORY:** Energies: Light

Jon Kent's genetics are unique. He is a naturally born human-Kryptonian hybrid, the son of Lois Lane and Superman (Kal-El/Clark Kent). As a consequence, no matter how much his parents attempt to provide Jon with a normal childhood, the development of his powers as he grows is a subject of intense interest, both among enemies and allies.

Family friend Batman has theorized that Jon's powers may even exceed those of his incredibly powerful father. As Jon reaches maturity, it has become apparent that even though only half his DNA is Kryptonian, he has all the same powers as his father. Like Superman, Jon is able to convert the energy from Earth's yellow sun into a vast range of incredible abilities.

MON-EL

REAL NAME: Lar Gand **POWERS:** Super-strength, speed, durability, stamina; heightened senses; flight; heat vision; freeze breath **FIRST APPEARANCE:** *Superboy* #89 (Jun 1961) **SUBSIDIARY CATEGORY:** Energies: Light

Mon-El is a descendant of the Houses of El and Zod, living in the 31st century. He comes from Daxam, a colony planet founded by space-faring Kryptonians many centuries earlier. Daxamite biology is therefore very similar to Kryptonian, exhibiting the same powers under a yellow sun, although instead of being vulnerable to Kryptonite, they exhibit extreme physical reactions to lead. Mon-El later moves to New Krypton, a settlement founded by his great-grandfather Dru-Zod on a planet orbiting two yellow suns. Here, he and his family have the typical incredible power set of Kryptonians.

GENERAL ZOD

REAL NAME: Dru-Zod **POWERS:** Super-strength, speed, durability, stamina; heightened senses; flight; heat vision; freeze breath **FIRST APPEARANCE:** *Adventure Comics* #283 (Apr 1961) **SUBSIDIARY CATEGORY:** Energies: Light

Like his nemesis Superman, Dru-Zod is a native Kryptonian who gains powers when he absorbs the energy of Earth's yellow sun. He survives his home planet's destruction due to being banished to the Phantom Zone at the time. The discovery that he is phenomenally powerful when proximal to certain types of stars, feeds Zod's desire to dominate others and get revenge on the House of El, who he blames for his imprisonment. In addition to the powers that come naturally through his Kryptonian DNA, Zod also has a talent for combat and strategy that was honed in Krypton's military, where he rose to the rank of General.

ANCILLARY EXEMPLARS

Preeminent scientist and patriarch of Krypton's leading family and Superman's father, **Jor-El**, escaped the destruction of his home world at the last moment. In addition to his Kryptonian powers under a yellow sun, Jor-El acquired a staff that gave him the ability to manipulate reality and sense fluctuations in the timeline. He could also fire Kryptonite blasts from one eye, because of a fragment of Krypton that had punctured it during the disaster. However, Superman's mother **Lara Lor-Van** never left her home planet of Krypton, so under its red sun she had no superpowers. It is not just Kryptonian humans who have amazing powers—the El family dog, **Krypto**, brought to Earth via the Phantom Zone, also possesses them.

MARTIAN MANHUNTER

REAL NAME: J'onn J'onzz **POWERS:** Super-strength, speed, durability, reflexes, senses; shape-shifting; invisibility; phasing; telepathy; flight **FIRST APPEARANCE:** *Detective Comics* Vol 1 #225 (Nov 1955) **SUBSIDIARY CATEGORY:** Metagenetic Manifestation

5 Ba

M

Martian
Manhunter

J'onn J'onzz is the Martian Manhunter, a phenomenally powerful being and valuable member of the Justice League. He is a Green Martian and a law enforcement officer—a Manhunter—on Mars, but tragically is one of the last of his race after a plague known as H'ronmeer's Curse ravaged his world. The disease is carried telepathically, proving devastating to the Martians whose minds were all linked. J'onn only survives because his mind is shut off from the rest of his people before he can be infected. At the moment that his wife and child die in front of him, he is transported to Earth by a scientist, Dr. Erdel. Realizing that his Martian appearance might cause alarm on Earth, J'onn uses his shape-shifting abilities to assume the form of police officer John Jones.

NATURAL LEADER

Although J'onn has suffered great personal tragedy, it is instinctive for him to use his gifts to help others, and after working as a detective he becomes part of the Justice League, for a time serving as its leader. His power set is incredible even by the standards of his fellow League members, encompassing super-strength, speed, and durability, and also extending to invisibility and being able to phase through solid objects. In addition to all this, J'onn has the telepathy natural to Green Martians. His only major weakness is a pathological fear of fire, perhaps stemming from the fact that the plague that took his people causes its victims' minds to combust.

Martian Manhunter's mental abilities include being able to link all the minds of the Justice League so that they can have a virtual meeting, which he calls a psychic boardroom.

MISS MARTIAN

REAL NAME: M'gann M'orzz **POWERS:** Super-strength, speed, durability, reflexes, senses; shape-shifting; invisibility; phasing; telepathy; flight **FIRST APPEARANCE:** *Teen Titans* Vol 3 #37 (Aug 2006) **SUBSIDIARY CATEGORY:** Metagenetic Manifestation

Although her usual form is that of a Green Martian, M'gann M'orzz, a.k.a. Miss Martian, is actually a White Martian. Since White Martians are monstrous in appearance and have a terrifying reputation among humans, M'gann follows the advice of her uncle, Martian Manhunter, and appears as a Green Martian to reassure those she interacts with. She keeps this appearance up so consistently that even her Titans teammates have no idea of her true origins until she gets injuries so severe that her body cannot hold its shape any longer. Like her Uncle J'onn, M'gann has a range of powers due to her Martian physiology, including super-strength, speed, and durability, and various psionic abilities like telepathy and telekinesis.

GREEN MARTIANS

REAL NAME: Various **POWERS:** Super-strength, speed, durability, reflexes, senses; shape-shifting; invisibility; phasing; telepathy; flight **FIRST APPEARANCE:** *Batman* Vol 1 #41 (Jun 1947) **SUBSIDIARY CATEGORY:** Metagenetic Manifestation

Natives of the planet Mars call themselves Ma'aleca'andrans. Known by outsiders as Green Martians, they have a wide range of powers that are impressive compared to almost any other species in the universe. Green Martians are all connected as one with each other via their telepathic abilities, in what is known as the "Great Mind." Usually presenting as green in color and with a humanoid shape, their shape-shifting ability means that this appearance can be changed as the situation demands. They are a philosophical and cultured people, but their world is ravaged first by a terrible civil war with the White Martians, and then a plague that all but wipes them out entirely.

WHITE MARTIANS

REAL NAME: Various **POWERS:** Super-strength, speed, durability, reflexes, senses; shape-shifting; phasing; telepathy; flight **FIRST APPEARANCE:** *Justice League of America* Vol 1 #71 (May 1969) **SUBSIDIARY CATEGORY:** Metagenetic Manifestation

The appearance adopted by White Martians is thought to represent their culture—warlike and savage—and differentiates them from their Green counterparts. The two are originally the same species, but following interference from the Guardians of the Universe they are split into distinct groups to weaken them. White Martians appear hairless, with a pointed tail and six clawed limbs. In time, the Whites and the Greens clash in a brutal civil war, which sees the Whites defeated—despite their propensity for violence—and their survivors banished to the Still Zone. It is later discovered that Martians and humans were the component parts of a warrior race created by Perpetua, but they were forcibly separated after she is first defeated billions of years ago.

LEGION OF SUPER-HEROES

REAL NAME: Various **POWERS:** Various **FIRST APPEARANCE:** *Adventure Comics* Vol 1 #247 (Apr 1958)

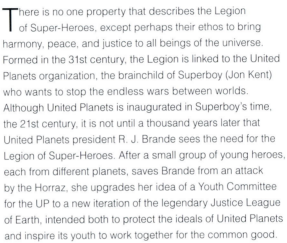

There is no one property that describes the Legion of Super-Heroes, except perhaps their ethos to bring harmony, peace, and justice to all beings of the universe. Formed in the 31st century, the Legion is linked to the United Planets organization, the brainchild of Superboy (Jon Kent) who wants to stop the endless wars between worlds. Although United Planets is inaugurated in Superboy's time, the 21st century, it is not until a thousand years later that United Planets president R. J. Brande sees the need for the Legion of Super-Heroes. After a small group of young heroes, each from different planets, saves Brande from an attack by the Horraz, she upgrades her idea of a Youth Committee for the UP to a new iteration of the legendary Justice League of Earth, intended both to protect the ideals of United Planets and inspire its youth to work together for the common good.

Each member of the Legion of Super-Heroes is a youthful being representing a single planet from the organization. This wide-ranging roster ensures a diversity of opinion and abilities, enabling the Legion of Super-Heroes to face any opponent with confidence and strength. While they are affiliated to the United Planets, autonomy of action is supposed to be included in the Legion's founding principles. This makes them politically independent and free to act without being led by factions that might form in their parent organization. They take as their base the city of New Metropolis on a fragment of what remains of Earth in their time. There, they live, train, learn, and eat together in a dining space called Heaven, where food from all member homeworlds can be found.

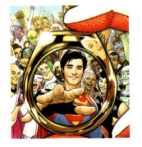

Each Legionnaire is issued a Legion Flight Ring made of Valorium, an alloy of the powerful Nth Metal. The ring gives the power of flight both through the atmosphere of planets and in outer space.

FOUNDING LEGIONNAIRES

The Legion's founding members are telepath Saturn Girl (Imra Ardeen), energy wielder Lightning Lad

(Garth Ranzz), and magnetism manipulator Cosmic Boy (Rokk Krinn). The trio quickly recruit the Coluan genius Brainiac 5 and the super-strong and durable Blok and Brainiac 5 is a key member of the Legion as his incredible intellect is the foundation for many of their mission plans as well as helping them get out of difficult situations. As the roster rapidly grows, the Legion uses a piece of tech called the Frichtman tag, which displays a readout over each member's shoulder of their codename, real name, home planet, and powers. While each member's power is usually different, all Legionnaires are issued with a Legion flight ring that enables them to fly—if they did not before—and serves as a visual reminder of their affiliation with the group.

While the Legion of Super-Heroes finds that it is not immune from being a tool of external agendas, its members always try to retain the spirit of optimism in which it was formed, the idea that the universe's youth can be empowered to bring about real change. They are the prime example of a way of working in which individuals from a wide range of backgrounds can come together and convert a multiplicity of strengths into one vision for the future.

STARFIRE

REAL NAME: Koriand'r **POWERS:** Super-strength, stamina, durability; energy blasts; flight
FIRST APPEARANCE: *DC Comics Presents* Vol 1 #26 (Oct 1980) **SUBSIDIARY CATEGORY:** Energies: Light

Princess Koriand'r, better known on Earth as Starfire, is from Tamaran, a planet whose inhabitants can process ultraviolet light in their bodies and convert it into energy that can fuel a variety of powers. Starfire can fly at high speeds even through the vacuum of space, and is super-strong and durable. When her planet is taken over by the cruel Citadel, Starfire is experimented on, a brutal process that leaves her with a further ability—being able to channel the energy she takes in and send it out through her hands as powerful blasts called Starbolts. It is unclear whether the experiments have given her the power, or whether her rage at her treatment caused a latent metagene to be unlocked.

WONDER TWINS

REAL NAME: Jayna and Zan **POWERS:** Metagenetic Manifestation **FIRST APPEARANCE:** *Extreme Justice* Vol 1 #9 (Oct 1995)

Twins Jayna and Zan come from Exxor, a planet where civilization has evolved to eliminate all societal problems. Both siblings have transformational powers but they manifest differently. Jayna can take the shape—and abilities—of any animal, while Zan can become water. Zan can even divide into multiple water molecules when the situation demands it—for example, to search several buildings quickly via the plumbing. Jayna studies thousands of animals from Earth and beyond so that she has a wide range of transformations to choose from at any given moment. However, the two can only use their powers by fist-bumping each other and saying out loud, "Wonder Twins powers, activate!"

PHANTOM GIRL

REAL NAME: Linnya Wazzo **POWERS:** When intangible is invulnerable, can pass through solid matter and fly
FIRST APPEARANCE: *The Terrifics* Vol 1 #1 (Apr 2018)
SUBSIDIARY CATEGORY: Metagenetic Manifestation

Linnya Wazzo, like her 31st-century descendant Tinya Wazzo of the Legion of Super-Heroes, is from the planet Bgztl. Like all Bgztlans, Linnya can become intangible and phase through solid objects. When in this state she can levitate and fly, is invulnerable, and has no need to eat or sleep. In their regular lives, Bgztlans can become intangible or solid as they wish, but when she is stuck in the Dark Multiverse, Linnya is trapped in her phantom form. This gives her the advantage of being able to survive for years until she is rescued. Her Bgztlan physiology means that she still ages even while intangible for long periods.

BRAINIAC

7   Vo

Br
Brainiac

REAL NAME: Vril Dox **POWERS:** Super-strength, speed, durability; high intellect; telepathy; advanced technology **FIRST APPEARANCE:** *Action Comics* Vol 1 #242 (Jul 1958) **SUBSIDIARY CATEGORY:** Genius Intelligence, Constructed Beings

Brainiac is classified as a 12th-level intellect, making him one of the most intelligent beings on his home planet Colu, a world of super-geniuses, and in his universe. Brainiac is phenomenally gifted in the field of robotics, enabling him to augment his natural abilities and intellect with artificial enhancements. As a cyborg, part organic and part mechanized, Brainiac's strength and durability are increased to the level that he is able to fight his nemesis Superman. He also designs and builds an army of drones to carry out his plans at a distance; his huge mental capacity allows him to command them with his mind. Another incredible technology developed by Brainiac is the mechanism for shrinking entire cities and preserving them in bottles.

BRAINIAC 5

14   Ba

Bv
Brainiac 5

REAL NAME: Querl Dox **POWERS:** Super-strength, speed, durability; high intellect; telepathy; advanced technology; flight **FIRST APPEARANCE:** *Action Comics* Vol 1 #276 (May 1961) **SUBSIDIARY CATEGORY:** Genius Intelligence

Like his infamous ancestor Brainiac, Brainiac 5 is a Coluan with 12th-level intellect. Unlike the original, however, Brainiac 5 uses his genius for good as a founding member and key part of the Legion of Super-Heroes in the 31st century. His brain works at a higher level than most beings, able to compute the probabilities of a situation using both scientific and emotional factors. This gives him a complete view of likely events in a way that virtually equates to seeing the future. Brainiac is thus extremely useful as a Legionnaire in assessing missions and deciding what action is needed, and he also uses his extensive scientific understanding to build equipment for the team to use.

ANCILLARY EXEMPLARS

37   Vo

Ch
Shade, the Changing Man

41   St

Sh
Shade, the Changing Girl

34   Vo

Ul
Ultra the Multi-Alien

Poet Rac Shade, a.k.a. **Shade, the Changing Man**, is from the planet Meta, and uses technology from his homeworld in the form of a reality-altering M-Vest that protects him and enables him to change his appearance. A fan of his called Loma, a birdlike alien, later takes his name in homage and comes to Earth as **Shade, the Changing Girl**, using a stolen M-Vest to inhabit the body of an Earth girl. **Ultra the Multi-Alien** is created using the genes of different alien races to bring harmony between them, but is kidnapped by a Thanagarian master criminal named Byth, wanting to use Ultra's various powers for evil.

LOBO

REAL NAME: Lobo **POWERS:** Super-strength, durability, stamina, senses; advanced healing factor **FIRST APPEARANCE:** *Omega Men* Vol 1 #3 (Jun 1983)

Lobo is one of the last surviving Czarnians, a race of super-strong aliens possessing an incredible healing factor that enables them to recover from almost any injury. A new Czarnian can even be regenerated from the smallest Czarnian cell, like a drop of blood. However, they can be killed by their own kind, and most meet their end at the hands of Lobo himself.

Lobo uses his considerable natural advantages to become one of the most feared yet sought-after bounty hunters in the universe. He prides himself on being a man of his word—he will pursue any contract to the end to carry out what he has promised to do—and is utterly ruthless. He has even managed to hold his own against the likes of Superman.

STARRO

REAL NAME: Star-ø **POWERS:** Mind control; self-duplication; regeneration; flight **FIRST APPEARANCE:** *The Brave and the Bold* Vol 1 #28 (Mar 1960)

Starro originates from an ø-world, a planet formed in a pocket within the universe where normal rules of reality do not apply. Although most creatures from such worlds rapidly become extinct, Starro thrives, eliminating all other life on its world and setting its sights on further conquests. Resembling an Earth starfish, Starro's main weapon is its ability to produce spores—smaller versions of itself—that attach onto the faces of other beings and take over their minds. Like others of his kind, Starro has evolved to bond with the lipocytes, the fatty tissue of the brain, "infecting" it until all that remains within the victim's consciousness is the will of Starro. Since Starro can regenerate from a fragment of itself, it is essentially immortal.

MONGUL

REAL NAME: Mongul **POWERS:** Super-strength, durability, stamina, speed, reflexes; healing factor **FIRST APPEARANCE:** *DC Comics Presents* Vol 1 #27 (Nov 1980)

Mongul is a Warzoon, a savage people whose native planet is the grim Warworld. An early ancestor had killed an alien visitor to the planet and stolen his armored skin, along with a powerful yet mysterious jewel worn by the visitor. These new accouterments enhanced the Warzoon's natural might and brutality, and he took the name Mongul, meaning "strongest." This title would be passed down through a succession of his descendants, several of whom would try and measure their strength against Superman. Also passed down is Mongul's hunger for power and lust for blood. The latest bearer of the name is no different, and it could be said that tyranny and violence are nothing more than Mongul's natural instincts.

DESPERO

11	Co
De	
Despero	

REAL NAME: Despero **POWERS:** Super-strength, durability; telekinesis; telepathy; energy blasts **FIRST APPEARANCE:** *Justice League of America* Vol 1 #1 (Nov 1960)

Despero is from the planet Kalanor, and for long spells is also its tyrannical ruler. He is a powerful telepath, his incredible psionic abilities linked to the third eye in the center of his forehead. He can also use the eye to harness energy to blast out of his mouth in a deadly torrent of fire—the revered Flame of Py'tar. Despero's ability to control the Flame is what enables him to elevate himself above other Kalanorians. Following an attempt to use Nth Metal to launch an invasion of Earth, Despero is killed by Hawkman but is resurrected due to his contact with the mysterious element.

MISTER MIND

3	Vo
Mi	
Mister Mind	

REAL NAME: Maxivermis Mind **POWERS:** Telepathy **FIRST APPEARANCE:** *Captain Marvel Adventures* Vol 1 #26 (Aug 1943) **SUBSIDIARY CATEGORY:** Magic

A diminutive mindworm from the planet Venus, Mister Mind is a powerful telepath despite his size, being a repository of all the psionic abilities of the rest of his lost race. His mental power is so great that he is thought to be able to alter reality. Mister Mind increases his power by absorbing the contents of various spellbooks in the Library of Eternity, harnessing magic to add to his already formidable abilities. Mister Mind's capacity to influence the minds of others, coupled with his access to the mystical arts, means that it is hard to be sure exactly what is the truth about him and what is merely an illusion that he wants others to see.

ANCILLARY EXEMPLARS

38	St
Js	
Jemm, Son of Saturn	

29	Vo
Kj	
Kanjar Ro	

30	Vo
Jx	
Jax-Ur	

39	Vo
Lz	
Lor-Zod	

33	Vo
Qb	
Queen Bee	

Other telepathic aliens include **Jemm, Son of Saturn**, prince of a race created and based on the Martians, who tries to use his power for good. **Kanjar Ro** has no exceptional physical powers but uses advanced weapons technology in his plans for conquest. **Jax-Ur** is dubbed the Phantom Zone's most deadly prisoner after he destroys the populated Kryptonian moon of Wegthor, and **Lor-Zod** is actually born in the Zone to his parents Dru-Zod and Ursa. **Queen Bee**, a.k.a. Zazzala of the planet Korll, is an unusual being whose apian powers include flight, as well as the ability to control bees and produce hypnotic pollen.

KRYPTONIANS

REAL NAME: Various **POWERS:** None under red sun but under a yellow sun they possess super-strength, speed, durability, stamina, reflexes, senses; flight; heat vision; and freeze breath **FIRST APPEARANCE:** *Action Comics* Vol 1 #1 (Jun 1938) **SUBSIDIARY CATEGORY:** Energies: Light

The biology of the people of Krypton is one of the wonders of the universe. Under their native red sun, they have no unusual abilities, but those few that manage to explore the wider reaches of space discover that they can absorb the energy of a yellow sun and convert it into a range of incredible powers, like super-strength, super-speed, heat vision, and freeze breath, among others. While outwardly they may appear very similar to Earth's people, Kryptonians' inner bodily structure contains organs that have no human equivalent, and help them to store and utilize vast amounts of energy. Before their planet is destroyed, Kryptonians are a highly advanced society, although their hierarchical structure is so rigid and limiting that it prevents them from addressing their impending doom until it is too late.

THANAGARIANS

REAL NAME: Various **POWERS:** Enhanced stamina, durability, and senses; access to Nth Metal grants flight, accelerated healing—limit and range of properties not yet known **FIRST APPEARANCE:** *The Brave and the Bold* Vol 1 #34 (Mar 1961) **SUBSIDIARY CATEGORY:** Metals

The planet Thanagar is the source of Nth Metal, an incredible element that leads the Thanagarians to learn how to defy gravity. Using the metal, they construct hawklike wings, although in fact any wearable item made from Nth Metal enables flight. Similarly, Thanagarian spacecraft are constructed from the metal. Those Thanagarians who have learned to master Nth Metal in greater depth have found a range of additional benefits, such as advanced healing to the point of limb regrowth, energy storage and conversion, and even time travel. Although they superficially resemble Earth humans, Thanagarians are more durable and longer lived, and also possess enhanced vision and hearing similar to the birds they imitate.

RANNIANS

8	St
Rn	
Rannians	

REAL NAME: Various **POWERS:** None; technologically advanced **FIRST APPEARANCE:** *Showcase* Vol 1 #17 (Dec 1958) **SUBSIDIARY CATEGORY:** Amazing Armor and Wondrous Weapons

Natives of the planet Rann are very similar to Earth humans, and close enough genetically for a child to be born to Rannian and human parents. Rannians are very technologically advanced, with their most remarkable innovation being the Zeta Beam, a form of instant intergalactic transportation. This highly useful invention enables Rannians to make contact with other peoples around the galaxy, but also makes them a target for those who want to repurpose it for their own nefarious ends. Rannians themselves are not a warlike race, leaving them vulnerable to attack from more belligerent alien species, like the Thanagarians.

DAXAMITES

16	St
Dx	
Daxamites	

REAL NAME: Various **POWERS:** None under red sun; under yellow sun: super-strength, speed, durability, stamina, reflexes, senses; flight; heat vision; freeze breath **FIRST APPEARANCE:** *Superboy* Vol 1#89 (Jun 1961) **SUBSIDIARY CATEGORY:** Energies: Light

Daxamites are descended from Kryptonian colonists and share many of their physical traits, including superpowers triggered by a yellow sun. Having eradicated the Kryptonians' natural weakness to Kryptonite, they are, however, adversely affected by exposure to lead. They also share the Kryptonians' vulnerability to magic. Many Daxamites adopt an isolationist policy, believing themselves to be a superior race, but some have reached out to other peoples. Daxam orbits a red sun, and Daxamites on their homeworld have no special powers, but those who travel to yellow star systems are enormously powerful.

ANCILLARY EXEMPLARS

36	Vo
Dm	
Dominators	

40	Vo
Re	
The Reach	

28	Vo
Du	
Durlans	

31	Vo
Ax	
Appellaxians	

32	Vo
Gi	
Gil'Dishpan	

35	Vo
Kh	
Khund	

The **Dominators** use their scientific genius to try and stamp out Earth's metahumans. The insectoid beings of **The Reach** build biological "scarab" weapons to infiltrate other worlds. The **Durlans** can shape-shift, while the

Appellaxians are varied in form. The power-hungry **Gil'Dishpan**, or Gil'Dan, resemble space-faring aquatic creatures, usually contained within a protective sphere, and the **Khunds** are known for their belligerence and love of war.

SPHERE OF THE GODS

Beings connected to the gods or the realm of magic are often the most powerful of all, with those linked to the higher powers of creation deemed supreme.

Dv DIVINE

The Amazons derive their awe-inspiring powers from the gods of ancient Olympus.

6 St **W** Wonder Woman	14 Ba **Dt** Donna Troy	37 St **Wg** Wonder Girl (Cassie Sandsmark)	39 St **Ya** Wonder Girl (Yara Flor)	7 St **Hi** Hippolyta	36 St **As** Artemis of Bana-Mighdall	28 St **Nu** Nubia

Mg MAGICAL

Magic-wielders operate in the shadows, in a realm where the edges of science are blurred.

						1 St **Sz** Shazam!
13 St **Za** Zatanna	8 Co **Ad** Black Adam	5 Ba **Fm** Shazam! Family	34 Vo **Cn** Constantine	15 Vo **En** Enchantress	4 St **Dc** Doctor Fate (Kent Nelson)	38 St **Fa** Doctor Fate (Khalid Nassour)
30 St **Xa** Madame Xanadu	29 Vo **Kl** Klarion the Witch Boy	41 Vo **Hm** Homo magi	40 St **Zt** Zatara	58 St **Tr** Traci 13	43 St **Hh** H-Dial	55 Ba **Dy** Dannyland
32 Vo **Hc** Hecate	9 Vo **Ci** Circe	2 Vo **Ts** Doctor Sivana	11 Vo **Fx** Felix Faust	49 Vo **Fy** Morgaine le Fey	51 Vo **Ms** Doctor Mist	57 St **Mv** Manitou Raven

NEW GODS

On the planets of New Genesis and Apokolips are found beings so powerful as to appear divine.

 17 Vo **D** Darkseid

 22 St **Mr** Mister Miracle

 25 St **Bi** Big Barda

 20 St **Hf** Highfather

 21 St **Mb** Metron

 19 St **Li** Lightray

 23 Vo **Da** DeSaad

 26 Vo **Sx** Steppenwolf

 18 St **Or** Orion

 24 Vo **Ff** Granny Goodness/ The Female Furies

 47 Vo **Kb** Kalibak

 48 Vo **Gy** Glorious Godfrey

 59 Vo **Al** Grail

DEMONIC

Those empowered by demons can achieve great things, but the cost can also be great.

 31 St **R** Raven

 27 Co **Et** Etrigan the Demon

 33 St **Dv** Blue Devil

 35 Co **Lu** Lucifer Morningstar

 52 Co **Tn** Trigon

 56 Co **Nn** Neron

 53 Vo **Ps** Psimon

 46 Co **Ed** El Diablo

HIGHER POWERS

Some beings are so transcendent as to defy explanation, connected with energies far older than the Multiverse itself.

  3 St **Cg** The Spectre

 16 St **Dn** Deadman

 12 Vo **Ec** Eclipso

 10 St **Ju** The Phantom Stranger

 50 Vo **Oc** Lords of Order and Chaos

 45 St **Hw** Hawk and Dove

 54 St **Dr** Dream

 44 St **Rk** Rama Kushna

 42 St **Pr** The Presence

WONDER WOMAN

REAL NAME: Diana of Themyscira **POWERS:** Super-strength, speed, durability, stamina, reflexes, agility, senses; flight; accelerated healing; immortality; animal communication **FIRST APPEARANCE:** *All-Star Comics* Vol 1 #8 (Jan 1942) **SUBSIDIARY CATEGORY:** Metagenetic Manifestation, Amazing Armor and Wondrous Weapons

The gods of Olympus occupy a separate, rarefied world from that of humans. Immortal and unimaginably powerful, they are largely indifferent to the petty troubles of ordinary people. Perhaps it is because Wonder Woman is "only" a demigoddess, with one divine parent, that she is not the same. She is dedicated to the pursuit of the truth, and is a warrior protecting those who cannot protect themselves.

Wonder Woman is born Diana of Themyscira on a mysterious island hidden away from the rest of the world. Her mother is Hippolyta, Queen of the Amazons, and Diana is brought up among that fierce tribe of warrior women. The Amazons are a race created by the goddesses of Olympus to protect Earth, mixing mortal souls with immortal energies to create a group of exceptional women.

At first believing that she is created from clay using magic, Diana later learns that she actually has a father—the mighty

Wonder Woman's most famous weapon is the Lasso of Truth, which can only be wielded by the pure of heart. It can compel someone to obey her command, and can also free someone from mind control by returning them to the "truth" of themselves.

Zeus. It is perhaps this dual heritage of god and Amazon that gives Diana a natural ability as a fighter. Honing her skills in the training arena, she becomes Themyscira's greatest warrior and is chosen to be the champion and ambassador of the Amazons in the world of mortals. For this role, she is given the Lasso of Truth, better known by the Amazons as the Golden Perfect, forged by the gods to be used only by someone pure of heart. With this, Diana is able to restrain opponents as well as render them unable to lie. She also wears bracelets made of the divine and virtually indestructible Eighth Metal, held together with another hard metal, Amazonium.

DIVINE INSPIRATION

While Diana's many strengths and abilities are natural consequences of her extraordinary physiology—and some incredible Amazonian artifacts—she also has additional powers bestowed upon her by her divine relatives in Olympus. Diana is known as a demigoddess and many of her close relatives are gods, but in reality this is just the way that the human mind has chosen to perceive and rationalize them. In fact, the so-called gods are extradimensional beings whose physiology is far superior to most other entities. Thus it is possible to talk about the biology of a god as something that human science has not yet been able to fully understand, but it is something that one day might be known in greater detail. It is thought that many beings worshipped as gods across the universe were once ordinary mortals, transformed billions of years ago by a pulse of cosmic energy called the Godwave.

Wonder Woman is both a pure symbol of love and truth and a hardened warrior who is the first to leap into battle and fight for what is right. She sees her mission as bringing peace and happiness to the troubled world beyond the boundaries of her blessed island.

DONNA TROY

REAL NAME: Donna Troy **POWERS:** Super-strength, speed, durability, stamina, reflexes, agility, senses; flight; accelerated healing; immortality; animal communication **FIRST APPEARANCE:** *The Brave and the Bold* Vol 1 #60 (Jul 1965) **SUBSIDIARY CATEGORY:** Magic

To an observer, Donna Troy seems to have all the powers of a born Amazon, just like Wonder Woman. But biologically, Donna is not like the Amazons. She is not born of flesh and blood, but shaped from clay by the witch Derinoe, her form imbued with magic. Created as a living weapon to bring down Wonder Woman and the other Amazons, Donna is instead rescued by them. Wishing to allow her a chance at a normal life, the Amazons implant false memories into Donna's mind, enabling her to go on to become a hero, part of The Titans team. In addition to all her powers, Donna carries the Lasso of Persuasion, an indestructible artifact that can force anyone it binds to obey her.

WONDER GIRL

REAL NAME: Cassie Sandsmark **POWERS:** Super-strength, speed, durability, stamina, reflexes, agility, senses; flight; accelerated healing; immortality; animal communication **FIRST APPEARANCE:** *Wonder Woman* Vol 2 #105 (Jan 1996) **SUBSIDIARY CATEGORY:** Metagenetic Manifestation

Cassie Sandsmark is Wonder Girl. She believes her powers are derived from a unique suit of armor until she discovers that she is the granddaughter of Zeus and the niece of Wonder Woman. Her armor is forged in the heart of a star and is invisible until the wearer chooses to reveal it. It also manifests a red lasso that channels energy. However, due to its enchanted nature, the armor can take control of Cassie unless she uses her willpower to keep it at bay. She also wields a diamond blade given to her by Zeus. Unlike Wonder Woman, Cassie's mother is human, but her powers are still extremely formidable thanks to her connection to Zeus.

WONDER GIRL

REAL NAME: Yara Flor **POWERS:** Super-strength, speed, durability, stamina, reflexes, agility, senses; hydrokinesis **FIRST APPEARANCE:** *Future State: Wonder Woman* #1 (Jan 2021) **SUBSIDIARY CATEGORY:** Metagenetic Manifestation

Yara Flor is born of an Amazon mother from Themyscira and a father who is a Brazilian river god. She and her mother are taken in by a tribe of warrior women called the Esquecida. When she is a young woman, Yara is taken to Mount Olympus as the protégé of the goddess Hera, where she is trained in combat by the centaur Chiron, given a sword by Hephaestus, and tutored in more cerebral arts like languages and philosophy by the god Eros. Although at first she struggles to keep calm and control her powers, bonding with a wild winged horse she names Jerry enables her to move forward take her skills to the next level. She also wields golden *boleadoras*, a weapon given to her by a water goddess.

HIPPOLYTA

REAL NAME: Hippolyta **POWERS:** Super-strength, speed, durability, stamina, reflexes, agility, senses; flight; accelerated healing; immortality; animal communication **FIRST APPEARANCE:** *All-Star Comics* Vol 1 #8 (Jan 1942)

Hippolyta is the leading Amazon, and, along with her sister Antiope, is the first to arrive on the Paradise Island of Themyscira. Hippolyta is born, or more accurately reborn, from the Well of Souls, a conduit built by the goddesses of Olympus to turn the souls of women killed by violence in the world of mortals into new beings—the fierce Amazons. As the Queen of the Amazons, Hippolyta's physiology is beyond that of any human in terms of strength and durability, and represents something of a bridge between humans and gods. She is also a formidable warrior, but although immortal in the sense that she will never die of old age, she can be harmed by the gods.

ARTEMIS OF BANA-MIGHDALL

REAL NAME: Artemis **POWERS:** Super-strength, speed, durability, stamina, reflexes, agility, senses; accelerated healing, immortality **FIRST APPEARANCE:** *Wonder Woman* Vol 2 #90 (Sep 1994)

Artemis is from the splinter tribe of Amazons known as the Bana-Mighdall. Disillusioned by what they saw as the Olympian gods' betrayal, a group of Amazons, led by Antiope, left Themyscira and embarked on a nomadic lifestyle, eventually settling in Egypt. They are a more belligerent people than the Themysciran Amazons, and Artemis is among their finest warriors. As her personal weapons, she has wielded the Lasso of Submission, bestowed upon her by Wonder Woman, and the divine Bow of Ra. The Bow is the signature weapon of whoever holds the title of Champion of the Bana-Mighdall, known as the Shim'Tar, and can be summoned at any time by the champion.

NUBIA

REAL NAME: Nubia **POWERS:** Super-strength, speed, durability, stamina, reflexes, agility, senses; accelerated healing; immortality **FIRST APPEARANCE:** *Wonder Woman* Vol 1 #204 (Jan 1973)

Formerly the appointed guardian of Doom's Doorway, a portal to Hades in Themyscira, Nubia later becomes Queen of all the Amazons after Hippolyta's abdication. She is born through the Well of Souls on the same day that Princess Diana (Wonder Woman) is born to Hippolyta, so the two think of themselves as sisters even more so than is usual for Amazons. In her previous life, she was a warrior princess of Madagascar. Her long years in the proximity of Doom's Doorway have given her an extra sensitivity for magic. As queen, she is blessed by the goddesses Athena, Aphrodite, and Hestia with a divine gem that is made into the Staff of Understanding. The Staff can either be used in its original form as a melee weapon or transformed into a lasso.

SHAZAM!

Sz

Shazam!

REAL NAME: Billy Batson **POWERS:** Advanced wisdom, super-strength, stamina, durability, speed; lightning manipulation; magic wielding **FIRST APPEARANCE:** *Whiz Comics* Vol 1 #2 (Feb 1940) **SUBSIDIARY CATEGORY:** Divine, Energies: Light

Billy Batson is an ordinary human, a troubled boy who has lost his parents and is being shuttled between foster homes, when his life changes forever. First, he is placed with kind and loving foster parents who already have several children in their care—a ready-made family—and second, he is chosen as the Champion of Magic by a dying wizard. Both of these events will have a transformative effect on Billy.

At a time when the hidden realm of Magic is in desperate need of a new Champion, its gateway, the Rock of Eternity, allows itself to be found, and it is Billy who comes through its doors. He meets an ancient man, the last survivor of the seven members of the Council of Eternity who swore to protect all magic. This wizard is unimpressed by Billy's appearance, but on closer inspection of his character he realizes that the boy is agitated but courageous, standing up for the weak against bullies, and that he has marvelous potential. The choice is made, and the wizard passes on his powers to Billy.

The Rock of Eternity where Billy acquires the powers of Shazam! is a conducting point for the magical energy known as the Living Lightning.

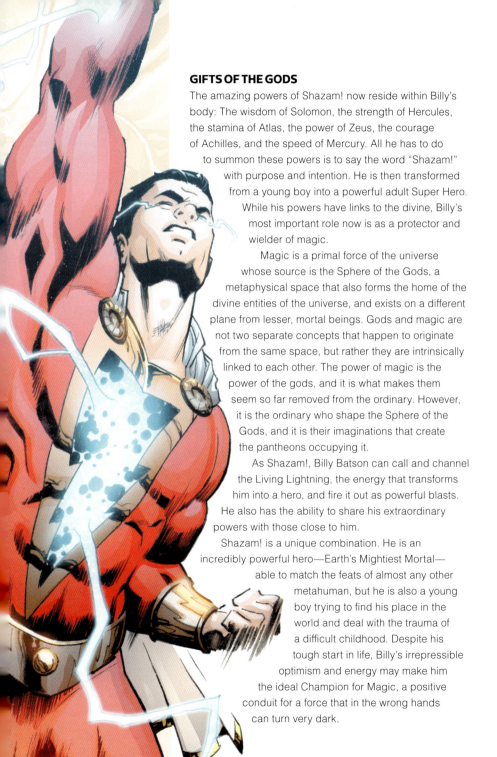

GIFTS OF THE GODS

The amazing powers of Shazam! now reside within Billy's body: The wisdom of Solomon, the strength of Hercules, the stamina of Atlas, the power of Zeus, the courage of Achilles, and the speed of Mercury. All he has to do to summon these powers is to say the word "Shazam!" with purpose and intention. He is then transformed from a young boy into a powerful adult Super Hero. While his powers have links to the divine, Billy's most important role now is as a protector and wielder of magic.

Magic is a primal force of the universe whose source is the Sphere of the Gods, a metaphysical space that also forms the home of the divine entities of the universe, and exists on a different plane from lesser, mortal beings. Gods and magic are not two separate concepts that happen to originate from the same space, but rather they are intrinsically linked to each other. The power of magic is the power of the gods, and it is what makes them seem so far removed from the ordinary. However, it is the ordinary who shape the Sphere of the Gods, and it is their imaginations that create the pantheons occupying it.

As Shazam!, Billy Batson can call and channel the Living Lightning, the energy that transforms him into a hero, and fire it out as powerful blasts. He also has the ability to share his extraordinary powers with those close to him.

Shazam! is a unique combination. He is an incredibly powerful hero—Earth's Mightiest Mortal— able to match the feats of almost any other metahuman, but he is also a young boy trying to find his place in the world and deal with the trauma of a difficult childhood. Despite his tough start in life, Billy's irrepressible optimism and energy may make him the ideal Champion for Magic, a positive conduit for a force that in the wrong hands can turn very dark.

ZATANNA

REAL NAME: Zatanna Zatara **POWERS:** Wields magic with almost limitless possibilities of shaping reality, both in her personal sphere and Multiversally **FIRST APPEARANCE:** *Hawkman* Vol 1 #4 (Nov 1964) **SUBSIDIARY CATEGORY:** Metagenetic Manifestation

Zatanna is the leading exemplar of the *Homo magi* strand of human evolution, those people who are genetically predisposed to an ability to access and wield magical power. She is born to two sorcerers, Sindella and the famous stage magician Giovanni Zatara. From her father, Zatanna learns both the art of performing magic to an audience, and how to protect this wondrous yet dangerous power on Earth. Despite the endless potential risks of using magic, Zatanna sees it as a precious commodity, without which the world would contain no wonder, no miracles.

As Zatanna grows to adulthood, she spends every waking hour training in the use of magic so that she can become its protector. It is vital that wielders of magic recognize the reality of this primal energy, and that all good magic has a dark equivalent somewhere—its natural law dictates that there must be a balance.

THE SCIENCE OF MAGIC

Zatanna is particularly adept at the art of logomancy—casting spells by speaking words backward. An incantation style such as this, or an enchanted object, is one of the external keys to achieving "magic sensitivity," and makes magic appear closer to a science, with its formulas and lab equipment. It is the inherent belief that magic exists and can be used to shape reality that is the main barrier to non-*Homo magi* accessing magic. For Zatanna, though, magic is as valid as any other branch of science or natural phenomena, and she uses it to fight against the most bizarre and otherworldly of threats as part of the Justice League and Justice League Dark.

Along with almost boundless abilities, Zatanna's incantations give her the power to fire visible magical energy through her hands.

BLACK ADAM

REAL NAME: Teth-Adam **POWERS:** Super-strength, stamina, speed; wisdom; lightning manipulation; healing; immortality; magic wielding **FIRST APPEARANCE:** *Marvel Family* Vol 1 #1 (Dec 1945)

Black Adam is the protector—some would say tyrannical ruler—of the ancient kingdom of Kahndaq, in the deserts close to Egypt. He is not born to royalty, but is taken into slavery as a child 5,000 years ago. His life is shaped by brutality and he loses most of his family. This trauma leads him to seize the opportunity to wreak his revenge— when his young nephew is granted the powers of Shazam! by a wizard and shares them with Adam, Adam kills the boy and takes all the power for himself. Later judged unworthy of these gifts, he is banished to the far side of the universe, where he remains for millennia.

GODS OF EGYPT

Eventually escaping, only to be killed in a battle with Shazam! (Billy Batson), Black Adam is resurrected by a group of Kahndaqi freedom fighters desperate to overthrow an oppressive regime. On this occasion, Adam does not gain powers from the same gods as before, but instead from Egyptian deities: the stamina of Shu, the speed of Horus, the strength of Amon, the wisdom of Zehuti, the light of Aten, and the resilience of Mehen.

As well as these magical enhancements, Adam has also spent his long life acquiring other skills, like proficiency in ancient martial arts. He sees himself as the liberator of Kahndaq, and has often clashed with heroes in his pursuit of power and his resolute mission to safeguard his homeland from any external interference. However, after thousands of years, Adam is carrying much guilt over the deeds of his past, and redemption via a new path is something that he is willing to consider.

Black Adam wears a signet ring made of Nth Metal. He can use the ring to channel his powers, or even pass them on to another designated successor, who must put it on and say, "Shazam!"

SHAZAM! FAMILY

REAL NAME: Various **POWERS:** Various **FIRST APPEARANCE:** *Whiz Comics* Vol 1 #21 (Sep 1941)

One of the most remarkable features of the power that Billy Batson wields as Shazam! is the ability to share it with others, particularly those who can be counted as "family." This ability saves his life when he and his foster siblings are attacked by Black Adam, and Billy transfers his new power to his family. While they receive all the abilities he has, their power is diluted by how many are transformed at any one time—if six of them possess the power of Shazam!, each has it to one-sixth of the level of Billy alone.

FAMILY FIRST

When Billy first uses his power-sharing capability, he makes his five foster siblings into adult heroes like him, but since they have very different personalities, they have different strengths that come to the fore in the heat of battle. While eldest sister Mary Bromfield is affected in a similar way to Billy, Freddy Freeman's use of the Stamina of Atlas removes the effects of a chronic neurological disease he suffers from. Pedro Peña is turned from a shy boy into a super-strong, muscle-bound hero; the super-smart Eugene Choi is enhanced by the wisdom of Solomon to be able to communicate with machinery; and youngest family member Darla Dudley gains the Speed of Mercury. These children are proof that families don't have to be born into, but can be found and chosen. The Shazam! Family are empowered in every sense of the word by their bond with each other.

While the Shazam! Family have their powers they are adults, but when the battles are done they return to their natural appearances and ages.

CONSTANTINE

REAL NAME: John Constantine **POWERS:** Human mage adept in a variety of spell-casting that bestows a wide range of abilities **FIRST APPEARANCE:** *Swamp Thing* Vol 1 #37 (Jun 1985) **SUBSIDIARY CATEGORY:** Superior Talents

John Constantine is one of Earth's most adept wielders of magic, but he is not one of the *Homo magi,* the strand of human evolution that has sorcery laced through its DNA. Rather he is an ordinary *Homo*

sapiens who has devoted his life to the learning of the magic arts. Constantine has a particular affinity for dark and demonic magic, the practice of which usually comes at some personal cost; in fact, he has lost many people close to him due to his involvement in the occult. He is an expert at deception both with magic and without, considered to be the world's greatest con man, and has the uncanny ability to be in the right place at the right time. As well as his spell-casting skills, Constantine is an astute investigator and expert in the occult.

ENCHANTRESS

REAL NAME: June Moone **POWERS:** Sorceress capable of using magical energy for a wide range of abilities **FIRST APPEARANCE:** *Strange Adventures* Vol 1 #187 (Apr 1966)

The Enchantress is an extremely powerful yet volatile magic wielder who habitually operates through a host body. Her true origins are unknown, but given the scale of her magical abilities—including bringing the dead back to life, manipulating reality, and transforming any object into something else—it seems probable that she has come to Earth from another dimension. When untethered and in her true form she becomes dangerously unstable, and her twisted magic strikes out randomly to cause terrible, mindless damage. Her usual host is the human June Moone, an unassuming freelance graphic designer who struggles to keep the Enchantress under control. However, June knows that she must maintain that control or the Enchantress will cause carnage in the world. Fortunately, the Enchantress seems to dislike being separated from June.

DOCTOR FATE

REAL NAME: Kent Nelson **POWERS:** Magic wielding; flight; immortality **FIRST APPEARANCE:** *More Fun Comics* Vol 1 #55 (May 1940) **SUBSIDIARY CATEGORY:** Amazing Armor and Wondrous Weapons, Divine, Metals

Kent Nelson's powers come from an extraordinary enchanted artifact—the Helmet of Fate. The Helmet is inhabited by the Lord of Order Nabu, a member of a group of ancient and powerful magical beings whose purpose is to battle the universal forces of Chaos. One of the earliest discoverers of magic on Earth, Nabu realized that the force was far too potent to contain within his body, so he transferred a portion of it to the helmet. Nabu is also able to capture his soul in the helmet to allow him to live on after his mortal body failed. As Doctor Fate, Kent Nelson also wears the Cloak of Destiny and the Amulet of Anubis. He takes on Nabu's mission to maintain Order, and the ancient spirit residing within the Helmet of Fate acts as his guide.

DOCTOR FATE

REAL NAME: Khalid Nassour **POWERS:** Magic wielding; flight; immortality **FIRST APPEARANCE:** *Convergence: Aquaman* Vol 1 #2 (Jul 2015) **SUBSIDIARY CATEGORY:** Amazing Armor and Wondrous Weapons, Divine, Metals

The great-nephew of previous Doctor Fate, Kent Nelson, Khalid Nassour is also descended from ancient Egyptian pharoahs, which is why the Egyptian gods choose him to be the new bearer of the Helmet of Fate. The Helmet, created from an alloy of the powerful and mystical Nth Metal, has for many years been the dwelling place of the spirit of Nabu, one of the Lords of Order. However, this situation is flexible, and other deities can occupy the helm to send messages to Doctor Fate. When wearing the Helmet of Fate, Khalid is not only able to deploy a vast array of magical abilities, but he also receives glimpses of the future. On one occasion, when he is temporarily blinded, the helmet restores Khalid's sight when he puts it on.

MADAME XANADU

30	St
Xa	
Madame Xanadu	

REAL NAME: Nimue Inwudu **POWERS:** Various magical abilities including soothsaying; decelerated aging **FIRST APPEARANCE:** *Doorway to Nightmare* Vol 1 #1 (Feb 1978) **SUBSIDIARY CATEGORY:** Metagenetic Manifestation

Madame Xanadu is a *Homo magi* with an illustrious lineage. She is the half-sister of the legendary King Arthur and sister of Morgaine le Fey, and was taught the art of magic by the great wizard Merlin. After narrowly escaping entering Avalon, the island of the dead, Madame Xanadu is touched by that land's enchantments and stops aging. Over the centuries she lives an itinerant life, earning her way as a fortune-teller. One of her principal magical attributes is being able to see visions of the future, which she often interprets for others through the medium of tarot cards.

KLARION THE WITCH BOY

29	Vo
Kl	
Klarion the Witch Boy	

REAL NAME: Klarion Bleak **POWERS:** Various magical abilities including transmutation and necromancy **FIRST APPEARANCE:** *The Demon* Vol 1 #7 (Mar 1973) **SUBSIDIARY CATEGORY:** Otherdimensional

Klarion is from Limbo Town, a settlement on a world where the practice of dark arts is commonplace. Dissatisfied with his life and wishing to do something more with his talents, Klarion decides to explore the Multiverse further. He operates in somewhat of a gray area ethically, not really acting for the greater good but thinking about how he can get to where he wants to be. His powers work by being channeled through his familiar—a cat named Teekl who also has magical abilities—but originally come from a primal place, a part of Nature.

ANCILLARY EXEMPLARS

41	Vo
Hm	
Homo magi	

40	St
Zt	
Zatara	

58	St
Tr	
Traci 13	

43	St
Hh	
H-Dial	

55	Ba
Dy	
Dannyland	

Homo magi are a species of naturally magical humanoids that has existed since the dawn of humanity. They include **Giovanni Zatara**, a powerful sorcerer, and **Traci 13**, who can use magic to channel the energy of cities. By its very nature, the realm of magic includes some bizarre beings and artifacts. The **H-Dial** resembles an old-fashioned telephone dial, and gives anyone who dials H-E-R-O (4376) temporary superpowers. Danny is a sentient street that communicates via posters and signs. He later transforms into the amusement park **Dannyland**. His teleportation ability proves very useful to the Doom Patrol.

HECATE

REAL NAME: Hecate **POWERS:** Virtually unlimited magical power; immortality **FIRST APPEARANCE:** *Superman Family* Vol 1 #218 (May 1982) **SUBSIDIARY CATEGORY:** Divine

Hecate is one of the most important beings in the universe, created from the primary magical energy in the cosmos. She is the first being to occupy the Multiversal realm of the Sphere of the Gods, and she is the one who causes all the other gods and magical beings of Earth to exist there. Initially, she is a benevolent being, reveling in the possibilities of magic and bestowing portions of it to various civilizations on Earth, the center of the growing Multiverse. Eventually she agrees to marry Hades and join the pantheon of the gods of Olympus as the goddess of witchcraft. However, when these gods reject her, she rages with vengeful fury, allowing dark magic into the world. Her magical powers are supreme in the Sphere of the Gods, and even the other gods fear her.

CIRCE

REAL NAME: Circe **POWERS:** Various magical powers, including animal transformation; immortality **FIRST APPEARANCE:** *Wonder Woman* Vol 1 #37 (Sep 1949) **SUBSIDIARY CATEGORY:** Divine

Circe is a witch who specializes in turning people into animals, or animal hybrids, some of which she marshals to do her bidding as so-called Ani-Men. She is a demigod, the daughter of a sun god, and is given her magical power by the goddess Hecate. Bitter at the injustices dealt out to her by men, Circe frequently uses her powers to bring them down. However, after losing her soul in a deal with the devil, she spends thousands of years in a fruitless effort to win it back. She searches other dimensions by opening portals with her magic, and also by trying to use Pandora Pits—alchemical receptacles of all the evils of the world. Her magic is tremendously potent, and enables her to change her own shape and also transform other things into whatever she wishes. She often comes into conflict with Wonder Woman who, as an Amazon with connections to Olympus, knows Circe's history all too well.

DOCTOR SIVANA

2   Vo
Ts
Doctor Sivana

REAL NAME: Thaddeus Sivana **POWERS:** Ability
to see magical energy; genius intelligence **FIRST
APPEARANCE:** *Whiz Comics* Vol 1 #2 (Feb 1940)
SUBSIDIARY CATEGORY: Genius Intelligence

Genius scientist Thaddeus Sivana loses his
faith in science when it fails to save his
family, so he pursues magic in the hope of
better results. After he breaks into Black
Adam's tomb he is struck by the Living
Lightning, which damages his right eye
but enables him to see magical energy.
This new connection to magic begins to
overwhelm Doctor Sivana's physique, so he
searches for a way to stop his deterioration.
When mindworm Mister Mind takes up
residence in Doctor Sivana's ear, the
connection gives Sivana a variety of magical
abilities, including energy blasts, flight, and
superhuman strength and durability.

FELIX FAUST

11   Vo
Fx
Felix Faust

REAL NAME: Felix Faust **POWERS:** Various demonic
magical abilities; immortality **FIRST APPEARANCE:**
Justice League of America Vol 1 #10 (Mar 1962)

Dark magician Felix Faust wants to gain
access to the Books of Magic so desperately
that he bargains away his soul to a demon
to facilitate acquiring them. This apparently
spiritual bargain has very real physical
effects, though, and Faust's face takes on
a withered appearance. Making pacts with
demons in exchange for securing more
power on Earth is Faust's usual modus
operandi. In addition to possessing a
range of magical abilities, he has a special
connection to a group of hellish brothers
known as the Demons Three. Faust often
summons these ancient, demonic creatures
to Earth with an incantation to cause chaos
for its heroes.

ANCILLARY EXEMPLARS

49   Vo
Fy
Morgaine le Fey

51   Vo
Ms
Doctor Mist

57   St
Mv
Manitou Raven

Thanks to their abilities to wield magic,
many *Homo magi* live extremely long lives.
Morgaine le Fey has been practicing her
particular brand of dark magic since the
days of her legendary brother, King Arthur.
Doctor Mist is a powerful, immortal African
wizard. Formerly a medical doctor, he
turns to the magic of his ancestors when
his wife is killed in a civil war. When no spells
restore her to life, Mist ends up working
for A.R.G.U.S., the US government
agency operating in the metahuman field.
Manitou Raven is a 3,000-year-old
shaman who harnesses the tribal magic
of the peoples living on Native American
Apache land. After he dies battling evil,
his wife valiantly takes up his mantle as
Manitou Dawn.

DARKSEID

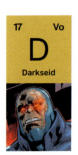

17	Vo
D	
Darkseid	

REAL NAME: Uxas **POWERS:** New God physiology gives super-strength, speed, intelligence, immortality; wields Omega Energy **FIRST APPEARANCE:** *Superman's Pal Jimmy Olsen* Vol 1 #134 (Dec 1970) **SUBSIDIARY CATEGORY:** Alien Origins, Genius Intelligence

The formidable Darkseid is one of the New Gods, a dynasty of deities whose rise comes when Darkseid kills his own father, the Old God Yuga Khan. He is acting to bring about a prophecy that the time of the Old Gods must come to an end, and the New Gods will take their place. The New Gods are immensely potent beings who live close to The Source, a reservoir of primeval energy connected to the beginnings of the universe. Most New Gods are considered to be the peak of evolutionary perfection, with exceptional strength, speed, and intelligence, and Darkseid is one of the leading exemplars of this. Following the downfall of the Old Gods, the two New God worlds of Apokolips and New Genesis are created, with Darkseid as the ruler of Apokolips. The entire realm of the New Gods is separated from the rest of the universe so that the only way it can be entered or left is via Boom Tube technology.

The world Darkseid calls home is a hellish planet of firepits and misery, where the population mostly consists of slaves. Order is maintained by his hordes of Parademons, and Darkseid also has a number of trusted councillors, military advisors, and bodyguards on hand.

Darkseid's Omega Beams are bolts of cosmic energy that can be fired from his eyes to devastating effect.

OMEGA ENERGY

As perhaps the most powerful and lethal New God in existence, Darkseid is a formidable opponent for virtually any hero. His most devastating weapon is the Omega Beam, which he channels from an energy he took from the Old Gods. This energy is fired from Darkseid's eyes in targeted beams that can track their victims in whichever direction they try to flee. As well as this more direct function, Darkseid also deploys this energy in a number of other ways: to create his own Boom Tubes at will for interdimensional travel, to fly, and for psionic abilities like telepathy and telekinesis.

Omega Energy has its origins in Anti-Life, the power to control the minds of sentient beings and both kill and resurrect them in an instant. This power is commonly expressed as a mathematical equation whose symbols represent various emotions and conditions like loneliness and despair. A being who masters the equation can wield its huge powers, and Darkseid intends to use it to conquer the entire universe.

Darkseid is a resolute entity who uses his extraordinary power for evil ends—the subjugation of any and all beings with whom he comes into contact. He is a force so great that he is capable of defeating even the mightiest member of the Justice League: only together do they have a hope of stopping him. Although he has been apparently killed before, he can be resurrected if his Omega Energy is transferred into a new body. If reborn as a baby, Darkseid can rapidly reach full strength again by absorbing energy from other godlike beings. While it is possible to briefly stop Darkseid when very powerful heroes work together, it seems that this Apokolyptian menace cannot be kept down for long ...

MISTER MIRACLE

REAL NAME: Scott Free **POWERS:** New God physiology gives super-strength, speed, intelligence, immortality; escapology **FIRST APPEARANCE:** *Mister Miracle* Vol 1 #1 (Apr 1971) **SUBSIDIARY CATEGORY:** Alien Origins, Genius Intelligence

Scott Free is a New God of New Genesis, son of its longtime ruler Highfather. In an attempt to broker peace between New Genesis and Apokolips, Scott is exchanged as a child with Darkseid's son Orion. His life growing up on Apokolips is a miserable one, although Scott does meet his future wife Barda there, and also perfects his escapology skills. As an elite New God, he has super-strength, speed, and intelligence, attributes he uses as the hero Mister Miracle when he escapes Apokolips and travels to Earth. Mister Miracle shows a particular aptitude with advanced New God technology like Mother Boxes, which are like sentient computers. As well as using Mother Boxes to travel via Boom Tubes, Mister Miracle can also move about on Aero Discs, flat circular gadgets that are placed under his feet for levitation and flight.

BIG BARDA

REAL NAME: Barda Free **POWERS:** New God physiology gives super-strength, speed, intelligence, immortality **FIRST APPEARANCE:** *Mister Miracle* Vol 1 #4 (Oct 1971) **SUBSIDIARY CATEGORY:** Alien Origins

Barda is the leader of the elite guards corps of Apokolips known as the Female Furies, until she falls in love with the captive Scott Free and joins him as he escapes from their home planet for Earth. As a New God, Barda possesses all the advanced physical attributes of that mighty race, in addition to her years of grueling military training at Granny Goodness's Orphanage facility. She also wields the Mega-Rod, which is both a tool and a weapon made from the same advanced technology as a Mother Box. The Rod can only be used freely by a being with a very strong will, as it is programmed to turn its users into unquestioning servants of Darkseid. Barda can deploy it as a melee weapon, or use it to create Boom Tubes for traveling around the universe.

HIGHFATHER

REAL NAME: Izaya **POWERS:** New God physiology gives super-strength, speed, intelligence, immortality **FIRST APPEARANCE:** *New Gods* Vol 1 #1 (Mar 1971) **SUBSIDIARY CATEGORY:** Alien Origins

Izaya the Inheritor is better known as Highfather, older brother of Darkseid and longtime ruler of New Genesis. As one of the pinnacles of New God evolution, Highfather is comparable in strength levels to his brother, but unlike Darkseid, he is the wielder of the Life Equation. This is a mathematical formula representing the importance of life and the need to preserve it. Despite this premise, the Life Equation can also be dangerous, giving users the ability to reshape reality at will. Highfather's pursuit of the Life Equation to stop his power-hungry brother led to him developing tyrannical traits that mirrored those of Darkseid.

METRON

REAL NAME: Metron **POWERS:** New God physiology gives super-strength, speed, intelligence, immortality; cosmic awareness via Mobius Chair **FIRST APPEARANCE:** *New Gods* Vol 1 #1 (Mar 1971) **SUBSIDIARY CATEGORY:** Alien Origins, Genius Intelligence, Amazing Armor and Wondrous Weapons

Metron is known as the God of Knowledge, the foremost mind among the intellectually advanced New Gods. He lives on New Genesis, spending his days in constant pursuit of knowledge and discovery. Metron uses the Mobius Chair created by the Anti-Monitor, which is one of the most advanced pieces of technology in existence. Sitting in the chair, he can travel through time and between dimensions, and is protected from virtually any attack. However, the chair's most impressive power is perhaps the immense knowledge it grants its user—virtual universal omniscience and a deep understanding of the cosmos. Metron's vast intelligence makes him an indispensable advisor to Highfather.

LIGHTRAY

REAL NAME: Solis **POWERS:** New God physiology gives super-strength, speed, intelligence, immortality; energy manipulation and projection **FIRST APPEARANCE:** *New Gods* Vol 1 #1 (Mar 1971) **SUBSIDIARY CATEGORY:** Alien Origins, Energies: Light

Lightray is a New God who, in addition to the natural advanced physique common to leading residents of New Genesis, has additional powers that he gains from the ability to absorb and convert solar energy. He can travel at around the speed of light—186,000 miles (299,337 kilometers) per second. Lightray can also fire out powerful energy blasts of light and heat, and even create miniature suns. His connection to light also means that he is able to detect separate parts of the spectrum. Lightray's personality matches his powers—he is a bright and sunny individual, unlike his best friend Orion, son of Darkseid, and is also a member of the Council of Eight, Highfather's military leaders.

DESAAD

REAL NAME: DeSaad **POWERS:** New God physiology gives super-strength, speed, intelligence, immortality **FIRST APPEARANCE:** *Forever People* Vol 1 #2 (May 1971) **SUBSIDIARY CATEGORY:** Alien Origins

DeSaad is Darkseid's trusted advisor and right-hand man on the planet of Apokolips. In addition to his naturally enhanced New God physiology, DeSaad can also absorb and control emotions. He can even trigger these emotions in others by using his psionic powers to control their minds, or create very convincing illusions to disorient them. This emotional vampirism also increases his power levels. DeSaad particularly thrives on negative feelings like fear and pain, and to that end he uses his flair for invention to create torture chambers for the hapless beings that fall under his sway. The information and leverage he extracts from these "skills" make him the ideal henchman for Darkseid in navigating the backstabbing world of Apokolyptian politics.

STEPPENWOLF

REAL NAME: Steppenwolf **POWERS:** New God physiology gives super-strength, speed, intelligence, immortality **FIRST APPEARANCE:** *New Gods* Vol 1 #7 (Mar 1972) **SUBSIDIARY CATEGORY:** Alien Origins

Steppenwolf is the uncle of Darkseid and one of Apokolips's foremost warriors. His military prowess is such that he can lead huge forces of the frenzied Parademons—genetically engineered, flying shock troops. He also trains and cultivates specially chosen warriors to be his elite squad, appropriately dubbing them the Hunger Dogs. Steppenwolf, along with other Apokolyptian forces, has also been known to ride on the backs of actual dogs—or rather giant alien creatures resembling canines—into battle. He himself wields an Electro-Axe, a formidable weapon that he floods with energy to enable it to cut through virtually anything. Like other New Gods, Steppenwolf does not need sustenance to survive, but he does enjoy the "idea" of food and drink.

ORION

REAL NAME: Orion **POWERS:** New God physiology gives super-strength, speed, intelligence, immortality **FIRST APPEARANCE:** *New Gods* Vol 1 #1 (Mar 1971) **SUBSIDIARY CATEGORY:** Alien Origins

Describing himself as the son of a monster, Orion is one of the children of Darkseid. His life is changed forever when he is made part of a "living peace treaty" between Apokolips and New Genesis, sent to live with the latter's ruler, Highfather. Orion is brought up as if he is Highfather's own son, shown the ways of peace instead of war, and taught to master his impulsive rage. Although he grows to be a loyal citizen of New Genesis, "war-born" Orion sometimes finds it hard to keep his aggressive Apokolyptian nature in check. His usual mode of transport is an Astro-Harness, which also allows him to fire blasts of an energy called the Astro Force.

GRANNY GOODNESS AND THE FEMALE FURIES

REAL NAME: Various **POWERS:** New God physiology gives super-strength, speed, intelligence, immortality **FIRST APPEARANCE:** *Mister Miracle* Vol 1 #2 (Jun 1971) **SUBSIDIARY CATEGORY:** Alien Origins

The Female Furies are Apokolips's most elite fighting force, trained by ruthless Darkseid loyalist Granny Goodness. Desperate to prove that the women of Apokolips deserve to be treated as well as the males, Granny Goodness pushes her charges to be better than anyone else, to fight twice as hard. Notable Female Furies include Big Barda, Lashina, Stompa, Mad Harriet, and Bernadeth, and all grow up in Granny Goodness' orphanage—part prison, part training facility for turning innocent children into brutal warriors. Although appearing well advanced in years, Granny Goodness is a mighty opponent herself, still retaining her natural New God strength.

ANCILLARY EXEMPLARS

The New Gods are a race of advanced beings that includes those who use their powers for peace and those who foment war. **Kalibak** the Cruel is one of the latter, a son of Darkseid and torturer of Apokolips. Using more subtle means of persuasion is fellow Apokolyptian **Glorious Godfrey**, who can influence the actions of others with his charisma and eloquence. However, **Grail** is different in origin. As the child of Darkseid and the Amazonian Myrina, she has a hybrid mixture of New God and Amazon physiology and powers. Additionally, Grail has knowledge of various Amazon occult rituals that allow her to transport her father Darkseid to wherever she is with dark magic.

RAVEN

REAL NAME: Rachel **POWERS:** Demonic heritage gives super-durability, astral projection, magical abilities; empath **FIRST APPEARANCE:** *DC Comics Presents* Vol 1 #26 (Oct 1980) **SUBSIDIARY CATEGORY:** Metagenetic Manifestation, Magical

Raven is born to a human mother, but her father is the demon Trigon. Raised by her mother to control her more demonic instincts, Raven tries to use her impressive power set for good. Her signature ability is the use of her Soul-Self, an astral projection consisting of dark energy and usually taking the shape of her human form or a large raven. While in this form, Raven can connect to other souls and exert a powerful influence over them. She can even use the Soul-Self to take hold of her physical body and those of others and teleport them. Raven is adept at using magic, another talent connected with her demonic heritage, but from her mother she inherits a strong empathic connection with others, being able to sense and affect the emotions of others.

ETRIGAN THE DEMON

REAL NAME: Etrigan **POWERS:** Super-strength and durability; immortality; hellfire blasts; magic **FIRST APPEARANCE:** *The Demon* Vol 1 #1 (Sep 1972) **SUBSIDIARY CATEGORY:** Magical

Etrigan is a rhyming demon from Hell, a follower of Lucifer. He has a rich demonic lineage, being the son of Belial, who is also the father of Merlin, and the grandson of Trigon. Even though he is a very formidable demon in his own realm, Etrigan needs a mortal host to manifest on Earth. This is frequently the human Jason Blood, whose soul is bound to Etrigan by Merlin. When he is in Etrigan's form, Jason benefits from all the advantages of a demon physiology, including super-strength and durability, advanced healing, immortality, and the ability to shoot hellfire blasts. To transform into Etrigan, Jason must intone a certain rhyming incantation. Despite Etrigan's demonic nature, Jason tries to use his considerable powers in a positive way. However, he cannot remain in Etrigan's form indefinitely, as Etrigan must return to Hell regularly to recharge his energies.

BLUE DEVIL

33 **St**
Dv
Blue Devil

REAL NAME: Daniel Cassidy **POWERS:** Super-strength, durability; flight; hellfire summoning **FIRST APPEARANCE:** *Fury of Firestorm* Vol 1 #24 (Jun 1984) **SUBSIDIARY CATEGORY:** Accidental

Daniel Cassidy had been merely an actor playing the part of a demon when he encountered the real thing, which cursed him to be bonded to his blue devil suit forever. Once reconciled to the changes in his life, Blue Devil decided that his next role would be that of a hero. The suit is in fact made from the skin of the demon Nebiros, so it has a variety of hidden attributes. It is fireproof and bulletproof, and when wearing it Daniel can fly and summon hellfire.
He also carries a large golden ax that can channel hellfire, and golden chains that he can send out to ensnare his opponents.

LUCIFER MORNINGSTAR

35 **Co**
Lu
Lucifer Morningstar

REAL NAME: Samael **POWERS:** Angel physiology gives wide range of powers, including flight, super-strength and durability; immortality; healing; magic; various psionic abilities **FIRST APPEARANCE:** *Sandman* Vol 2 #4 (Apr 1989) **SUBSIDIARY CATEGORY:** Metagenetic Manifestation, Magic

Lucifer is a fallen archangel, banished to Hell after starting a war in Heaven and being defeated by his brother Michael. Despite his banishment, he still has the physical attributes of an angel, including healing, cosmic awareness, the ability to travel between dimensions, enhanced senses, and also flight, even though his wings have been removed. For a time, Lucifer leaves Hell to open a bar in order to observe humans more closely. He is often able to tempt them into making deals with him in exchange for their souls, which then become his property in Hell.

ANCILLARY EXEMPLARS

52 **Co**
Tn
Trigon

56 **Co**
Nn
Neron

53 **Vo**
Ps
Psimon

46 **Co**
Ed
El Diablo

There are many demons eager to menace Earth and capture human souls. **Trigon** ascends to a greater level of demonhood after merging with a vast reservoir of evil collected from across universes, but his hunger for more evil is never sated. **Neron**, sometimes known as Satan or the Devil, is the ruler of Hell, and although he can be defeated and even apparently killed when he comes to Earth, he is forever reborn in Hell. **Psimon** is not a demon himself but is granted great psionic abilities by Trigon and becomes telepathic and telekinetic. Old West bank teller Lazarus Lane is inhabited by a spirit of vengeance to become **El Diablo**, using his demonic powers to stop the evildoers of his time and place.

THE SPECTRE

REAL NAME: Jim Corrigan **POWERS:** Near omnipotence and omniscience; immortality; psionic abilities; magic; rapid interdimensional travel **FIRST APPEARANCE:** *More Fun Comics* Vol 1 #52 (Feb 1940) **SUBSIDIARY CATEGORY:** Divine, Magical

Police officer Jim Corrigan is chosen to be The Spectre, the human host of the divine Spirit of Vengeance, Aztar. Since Aztar operates from a position of holy wrath, Jim's humanity is intended to balance this out and make The Spectre's actions in punishing the wicked less cruel. His connection to The Presence, the highest power in existence, means that The Spectre's own powers are near limitless. He is virtually omnipotent and can reshape reality at will. He is also nigh omniscient with almost total cosmic awareness, can travel anywhere in the Multiverse, and can fire eldritch energy. While he is one of the more supreme beings in the Multiverse, The Spectre is totally focused on bringing the wicked to justice, and has no interest in furthering any other personal ambitions.

DEADMAN

REAL NAME: Boston Brand **POWERS:** Intangibility; invisibility; possession **FIRST APPEARANCE:** *Strange Adventures* Vol 1 #205 (Oct 1967)

Deadman is a hero with a difference— he has already died. He is prevented from moving on by the goddess of karma, Rama Kushna, who wishes him to atone for his egocentric life and returns him to the land of the living as a spirit. His mission is to make the lives of others better. As Deadman, Boston Brand is a ghost who is unable to touch anything, but his main power is to possess living beings and compel them to do his bidding. He is also invisible and cannot be heard by most people, although some humans with stronger links to the magical and spiritual worlds can perceive and communicate with him. As a ghost, Boston is wearing the clothes and mask he was shot and killed in while performing a high-wire trapeze act in a circus. He also keeps his stage name of Deadman, coined to reflect the danger of his act.

ECLIPSO

REAL NAME: Kaala **POWERS:** Super-strength and durability; immortality; psionic abilities; dark energy manipulation **FIRST APPEARANCE:** *House of Secrets* Vol 1 #61 (Jul 1963) **SUBSIDIARY CATEGORY:** Divine

Eclipso is the spirit of God's wrath, formerly the instrument of divine vengeance until he became evil and was replaced by The Spectre. Captured and imprisoned in a black diamond called the Heart of Darkness, Eclipso still manages to spread his malign influence to whoever possesses that gem. He is able to take control of anyone who touches it, making his host body incredibly strong and durable, although he is vulnerable to sunlight and can be forced to retreat back into the gem after overexposure. His psionic powers are extremely advanced and extend to telekinesis, telepathy, and mind control.

THE PHANTOM STRANGER

REAL NAME: Judas Iscariot **POWERS:** Omniscience; immortality **FIRST APPEARANCE:** *The Phantom Stranger* Vol 1 #1 (Aug 1952)

The origins of The Phantom Stranger are shrouded in mystery, perhaps because he has existed for so long. Some say he has walked the Earth since its beginnings, others that he is Judas Iscariot, the betrayer of Jesus, condemned to roam until he has atoned for his great sin. What is known is that for thousands of years the Stranger has stood against the forces of evil, often those of magical origin. Seemingly no other being has the power to end the Stranger's existence, and though his own powers are thought to be near limitless, his modus operandi is not to intervene directly in situations but rather act as a guide to others.

ANCILLARY EXEMPLARS

The **Lords of Order and Chaos** are two opposing groups—beings of pure energy who use physical hosts. Two avatars of Order and Chaos have teamed up, their differing natures forging a perfect balance—**Hawk and Dove**. **Dream**, one of a group of powerful beings known as the Endless, personifies the world of sleep and rules over the Dreaming. **Rama Kushna** is the goddess of karma whose stronghold is the holy city of Nanda Parbat. **The Presence**, the creator and source of all things, is the one above all in the Multiverse.

FORCES OF THE UNIVERSE

The Multiverse contains energies that work together to create harmony. These forces are linked to and channeled by some of the most extraordinary heroes and villains in existence.

SPEED FORCE

The Speed Force is based on velocity, and is the power that moves reality and time forward in the Multiverse.

4 St **F** The Flash (Barry Allen)	**9** Ba **Fl** The Flash (Wally West)	**1** Ba **J** The Flash (Jay Garrick)	**13** Vo **Eo** Reverse-Flash (Eobard Thawne)	**6** Vo **Gg** Gorilla Grodd	**45** Vo **Tu** Turtle	**56** Tx **Nf** Negative Flash
49 Vo **Tt** Tornado Twins	**39** St **Kf** Kid Flash	**25** St **Im** Impulse (Bart Allen)	**29** St **Ir** Impulse (Irey West)	**42** St **Av** The Flash of China	**22** St **Jc** Jesse Quick	**52** St **Xs** Xs
53 St **Jw** Jai West	**46** St **Jq** Johnny Quick	**44** St **Mx** Max Mercury	**50** Vo **Lf** Lady Flash	**26** Vo **Sv** Savitar	**28** Vo **Zo** Zoom	**37** St **Rv** Reverse-Flash (Daniel West)
27 Vo **Df** Dark Flash	**41** Vo **Gs** Godspeed					

EMOTIONAL SPECTRUM

The emotional spectrum encompasses energy created by certain feelings and abilities generated by sentient beings in the Multiverse.

7 Vo	20 Ba	18 St	23 St	2 Ba	57 St	59 St
G	**Gl**	**Gu**	**Gk**	**Ga**	**Bz**	**Gj**
Green Lantern (Hal Jordan)	Green Lantern (John Stewart)	Green Lantern (Guy Gardner)	Green Lantern (Kyle Rayner)	Green Lantern (Alan Scott)	Green Lantern (Simon Baz)	Green Lantern (Jessica Cruz)

61 St	60 St	12 Vo	34 Vo	24 Vo	30 Vo	8 Ba
Sj	**Tl**	**Si**	**At**	**Px**	**Sk**	**Gc**
Green Lantern (Jo Mullein)	Teen Lantern	Sinestro	Atrocitus	Parallax	Soranik Natu	Green Lantern Corps

11 St	15 Vo	36 Vo	51 Vo	54 Vo	55 Vo	3 St
Gd	**Ka**	**Vo**	**Gt**	**Sy**	**Sc**	**Ss**
Guardians of the Universe	Krona	Volthoom	Ganthet	Sayd	Scar	Star Sapphires

32 Vo	33 Vo	31 St	21 Vo	43 Vo
La	**Wa**	**In**	**Nk**	**Ux**
Larfleeze	Saint Walker	Indigo-1	Nekron	Umbrax

LIFE FORCE

This energy spawns the existence of all beings, and is particularly strong in those with a connection to the ocean.

5 St	14 St	35 St	10 Ba	16 Vo	17 St	40 Vo
A	**Me**	**Aq**	**Te**	**Om**	**Ta**	**Co**
Aquaman	Mera	Aqualad	Tempest	Ocean Master	Tula	Corum Rath

38 Vo	19 St	47 Vo	62 St	48 St	58 St
Ne	**Do**	**An**	**Ac**	**Nv**	**Mu**
Nereus	Dolphin	Atlanna	Andy Curry	Nuidis Vulko	Murk

FORCES OF THE UNIVERSE:
SPEED FORCE

THE FLASH

4		St
F		
The Flash		

REAL NAME: Barry Allen **POWERS:** Connection to Speed Force gives super-speed, reflexes, durability, stamina, agility; advanced healing; time travel **FIRST APPEARANCE:** *Showcase* #4 (Oct 1956) **SUBSIDIARY CATEGORY:** Accidental, Genius Intelligence

Having suffered the trauma of losing his mother to murder as a young boy, Barry Allen devotes his life to the pursuit of justice. As an extremely talented scientist, especially in the field of chemistry, he finds his calling as a crime scene forensics investigator. However, while working cases in his lab one night, Barry's life takes an incredible turn when lightning strikes him through the window, causing him to spill a mixture of chemicals on his body. Barry is rendered comatose for months, and eventually wakes to find that he has the power of super-speed.

It is instinctive for Barry to investigate this strange new phenomenon in a scientific way, and he essentially turns his body into a crime scene to conduct a thorough examination of his newfound abilities. Blood samples reveal that the molecules of his body have been energized, while his metabolism has been accelerated to astounding levels. His heart rate is also heightened well beyond that of a normal human's. Experimenting with the practical applications of his

When young forensic scientist Barry Allen was struck by lightning and soaked in chemicals, it ignited a connection to the Speed Force, making him the ultimate Scarlet Speedster.

body's new properties leads Barry to discover that he can actually vibrate his molecules at such a frequency that he is able to pass through solid objects. However, the most amazing talent he has is his pure speed. At first afraid to push himself too fast and too far, Barry is soon running so quickly that he actually travels through time. The effects of his super-speed do not just manifest themselves physically. Barry's mental capacities also work at dizzying speeds, a tremendous boost to his already impressive investigative skills.

SPEED FORCE

As Barry comes to discover over time, the source of his power is one of the foundational energies of the universe—the Speed Force. This cosmic phenomenon is, to put it simply, behind all the forward motion that exists, both in terms of physical objects and time. When a being is connected to it, they are even able to enter the Speed Force as if it were a separate dimension. Not only that, but once there, it is possible to view and access different points in time and space. Some who have studied the Speed Force in detail believe that it seeks out certain individuals to act as conduits, and these chosen few must use their power to expend Speed Force energy almost as if they are releasing pressure from the system.

While Barry Allen's powers as The Flash are awe-inspiring, their sheer magnitude carries a permanent threat. When he discovers the true identity of his mother's killer (Eobard Thawne, a.k.a. Reverse-Flash), he travels back in time to stop the tragedy. This act apparently causes the fracturing of timelines and the disappearance of relationships and even people who are very important to Barry. It is later revealed that the true orchestrator of these events is an even more powerful individual than The Flash.

Barry Allen always carries the memory of his lost mother in his heart, but his unique blend of humanity, intelligence, and incredible super-speed enable him to be the protector of Central City and a symbol of hope for the future.

THE FLASH

REAL NAME: Wally West **POWERS:** Connection to Speed Force gives super-speed, reflexes, durability, stamina, agility; advanced healing; time travel; cosmic awareness **FIRST APPEARANCE:** *The Flash* Vol 1 #110 (Jan 1960) **SUBSIDIARY CATEGORY:** Accidental

Wally West is meeting his hero The Flash in Barry Allen's laboratory when, in what seems like a billion to one chance, he is struck by lightning and covered in chemicals in exactly the same way as Barry before him.

Like Barry, Wally now has a connection to the Speed Force and all the amazing powers that go with that. However, Wally's link to the universal energy is even stronger than Barry's, as he is trapped within the Speed Force for many years after the *Flashpoint* event, with his friends and family forgetting he had even existed. He can sense disturbances in the flow of time and reality by "tuning in" to the energy around him. Wally is also capable of running faster than Barry because his mind is naturally less analytical—he can allow himself to fully embrace the Speed Force.

THE FLASH

REAL NAME: Jay Garrick **POWERS:** Connection to Speed Force gives super-speed, reflexes, durability, stamina, agility; advanced healing; time travel **FIRST APPEARANCE:** *Flash Comics* Vol 1 #1 (Jan 1940) **SUBSIDIARY CATEGORY:** Accidental

In a sense, the father of all speedsters, Jason "Jay" Garrick is a World War II-era scientist whose connection to the Speed Force comes about through a lab accident. The extraordinary powers that he acquires

lead him to become the hero known as The Flash and he joins the Justice Society of America. Jay possesses super-speed and all the abilities that come with it, such as accelerated healing, enhanced senses, and time travel. However, timeline disturbances result in Jay becoming trapped within the Speed Force itself and his exploits are forgotten for many years. Eventually he is released and his history reinstated, and Jay is able to return to heroics along with perhaps his greatest power—being a wise mentor for younger speedsters.

REVERSE-FLASH

13	Vo
Eo	
Reverse-Flash	

REAL NAME: Eobard Thawne **POWERS:** Super-speed, reflexes, durability, stamina, agility; advanced healing; time travel, time manipulation; dimensional travel; cosmic awareness **FIRST APPEARANCE:** *The Flash* Vol 1 #139 (Sep 1963) **SUBSIDIARY CATEGORY:** Lab Created, Genius Intelligence

Twenty-fifth-century Flash obsessive Eobard Thawne managed to gain powers like his idol by harnessing residual traces of the Speed Force from one of Barry Allen's old costumes. However, his hero worship turns to hate, and he dedicates his life to punishing The Flash for his perceived transgressions against himself. Thawne's powers are different to most other speedsters as he is able to create and use the Negative Speed Force, which is more destructive than the Speed Force. He is faster than The Flash, and his travels through time and realities mean that he is more aware of the existence of other timelines, such as the *Flashpoint*, and their consequences.

GORILLA GRODD

6	Vo
Gg	
Gorilla Grodd	

REAL NAME: Grodd **POWERS:** Super-speed, strength, reflexes, durability, stamina, agility; telepathy; telekinesis **FIRST APPEARANCE:** *The Flash* Vol 1 #106 (May 1959) **SUBSIDIARY CATEGORY:** Natural World

Grodd is one of the remarkable apes of Gorilla City, whose long association with The Light—the apes' name for the Speed Force—gives them a profound understanding of this powerful energy. When Grodd spends time trapped in the Speed Force, its power causes him to evolve advanced telepathy, something usually only found among the elders of Gorilla City. With mental abilities greater than any of his kind, Grodd is the natural choice as the alpha—the leader—a position he cements in the traditional way by killing his father and consuming his brain to acquire his attributes. Unfortunately for humankind and unlike many of his kin, Grodd is power-crazed and warlike, with a particular enmity for The Flash, resenting his connection to the Speed Force.

ANCILLARY EXEMPLARS

45	Vo
Tu	
Turtle	

56	Tx
Nf	
Negative Flash	

49	Vo
Tt	
Tornado Twins	

Counterbalancing the Speed Force is the Still Force, a cosmic phenomenon of inertia that decelerates the kinetic energy of the universe. This is the source of the power of the **Turtle**, a foe of The Flash whose touch can take away the hero's speed. Speedster Meena Dharwan, meanwhile, is powered by the Negative Speed Force as **Negative Flash**, but when combined with the Speed Force it damages her body, and its ill effects are only held at bay by a power-dampening collar. Dawn and Don Allen are Barry Allen's children from the 30th century, who use their Speed Force powers for their signature move of creating powerful vortexes as the **Tornado Twins**. They are exploited by Reverse-Flash to fight against their father in the Legion of Zoom.

FORCES OF THE UNIVERSE: SPEED FORCE

KID FLASH

REAL NAME: Wallace R. West **POWERS:** Connection to Speed Force gives super-speed, reflexes, durability, stamina, agility; advanced healing; manipulates Speed Force to fire electric blasts; can tap into Speed Force power of others **FIRST APPEARANCE:** *The Flash Annual Vol 4* #3 (Jun 2014) **SUBSIDIARY CATEGORY:** Accidental

As a cousin of The Flash (Wally West), Wallace R. West is already a part of The Flash Family before he gets his Speed Force powers. Wallace's connection to that powerful universal force comes when a future version of himself transmits his own powers to him before dying. Although at first the young Wallace struggles to control the astonishing forces flowing through him, when he is struck by Speed Force lightning, his connection to it is taken up a notch and he becomes better able to channel it. Wallace also discovers that he is able to focus the Speed Force into electric blasts that he can fire out of his hands.

IMPULSE

REAL NAME: Bart Allen **POWERS:** Connection to Speed Force gives super-speed, reflexes, durability, stamina, agility; advanced healing **FIRST APPEARANCE:** *The Flash Vol 2* #91 (Jun 1994) **SUBSIDIARY CATEGORY:** Metagene Mutation

Bart Allen is Barry Allen's grandson from the future, having inherited his Speed Force powers. On his mother's side, he is also related to Barry's nemesis Eobard Thawne.

Bart thinks of himself as the most unique of all The Flash Family, because he has spent so long in the Speed Force jumping between different times and dimensions. This, added to the fact that his metabolism is hyperactive even for a speedster, means that he has lost track of how old he is. For a time, Bart becomes trapped in the Speed Force, and the exposure to it has given him an awareness of the many changes to the timestream and alternate realities that have existed.

IMPULSE

REAL NAME: Irey West **POWERS:** Connection to Speed Force gives super-speed, reflexes, durability, stamina, agility; advanced healing; ability to share Speed Force powers with others; dimensional travel **FIRST APPEARANCE:** *The Flash Vol 2* #225 (Oct 2005) **SUBSIDIARY CATEGORY:** Metagenetic Manifestation

As the daughter of The Flash (Wally West), Iris "Irey" West inherits a connection to the Speed Force that gives her amazing powers. Her happy family life vanishes in an instant when she is swept into the Dark Multiverse with her twin brother Jai, and the *Flashpoint* event causes their mother to forget them, while their father becomes lost in the Speed Force. When Irey and Jai are eventually freed and returned to Earth-Zero, Irey begins to eagerly embrace her powers, taking on the Impulse identity and becoming a full-fledged member of The Flash Family. As is common with speedsters, the Speed Force bestows an extra ability on Irey—in her case, to be able to transmit the Speed Force to someone else and temporarily empower them.

THE FLASH OF CHINA

42	St
Av	
The Flash of China	

REAL NAME: Avery Ho **POWERS:** Connection to Speed Force gives super-speed, reflexes, durability, stamina, agility; advanced healing **FIRST APPEARANCE:** *The Flash* Vol 5 #3 (Sep 2016) **SUBSIDIARY CATEGORY:** Accidental

Avery Ho's life is transformed when she is struck by lightning during a Speed Force storm in Central City. At first, the Chinese-American teenager is overwhelmed, having no idea how to control her incredible powers, but The Flash (Barry Allen) teaches her how to use a technique of focusing on the things she loves the most. This enables her to calm her rushing emotions and, by extension, her body. Later, Avery's skill set gets her invited to join the roster of the Justice League of China, where she delights in beating the fledgling Super-Man of China in a race.

JESSE QUICK

22	St
Jc	
Jesse Quick	

REAL NAME: Jesse Chambers **POWERS:** Connection to Speed Force gives super-speed, reflexes, durability, stamina, agility; advanced healing **FIRST APPEARANCE:** *Justice Society of America* Vol 2 #1 (Aug 1992) **SUBSIDIARY CATEGORY:** Transformative Science, Metagenetic Manifestation

The daughter of Golden Age speedster Johnny Quick, Jesse Chambers becomes trapped in the Speed Force after the reality-altering *Flashpoint*. She is later pulled out by The Flash (Barry Allen) to rejoin The Flash Family on Earth-Zero. Jesse accesses the Speed Force by using a scientific formula, 3x2(9YZ)4A, which she inherits from her father. This is deployed almost like a mantra, making Jesse's connection to the Speed Force both spiritual and highly analytical. Jesse's mother is also a Golden Age hero, Liberty Belle, from whom she gets her super-strength.

ANCILLARY EXEMPLARS

52	St
Xs	
XS	

53	St
Jw	
Jai West	

46	St
Jq	
Johnny Quick	

44	St
Mx	
Max Mercury	

50	Vo
Lf	
Lady Flash	

Other people with connections to the Speed Force include blood relatives like **XS**, granddaughter of Barry Allen from a possible future; **Jai West**, twin of Irey and son of Wally West; and Johnny Chambers, also known as **Johnny Quick** and father of Jesse. Speedsters originating from different times and realities include **Max Mercury**, the Zen master of speed from the early 19th century. **Lady Flash**, meanwhile, becomes the Russian version of The Flash after taking an experimental serum.

SAVITAR

REAL NAME: Unknown **POWERS:** Connection to Speed Force gives super-speed, strength, reflexes, durability, stamina, agility; advanced healing; time travel **FIRST APPEARANCE:** *The Flash* Vol 2 #108 (Dec 1995) **SUBSIDIARY CATEGORY:** Accidental

Savitar is a former pilot who is given Speed Force powers while flying an experimental plane. The self-proclaimed God of Speed wants to master the Speed Force totally, absorbing all of it into himself to attain ultimate power. Trapped in a void outside time, Savitar manages to tap into the Speed Force to create a portal and escape into it. Although he learns how to siphon the Speed Force while caught inside it, the Speed Force takes action to try and push him out, as an organism would a destructive parasite. However, Savitar has constructed an apparently unbreakable connection to it. The effects of this bond create dangerous Speed Force explosions, and Savitar is only stopped when The Flash (Wally West) manages to drain the Speed Force from him.

ZOOM

REAL NAME: Hunter Zolomon **POWERS:** Super-speed, strength, reflexes, durability, stamina, agility; advanced healing; time travel, dimensional travel **FIRST APPEARANCE:** *The Flash: Secret Files & Origins #3* (Nov 2001)

Hunter Zolomon's super-speed is not like other people's. After being paralyzed from the waist down, he tries to use the Cosmic Treadmill to travel in time and prevent the accident that injured him from happening. By doing this, he causes an explosion that grants him the power to alter time around himself, giving the effect of super-speed if he so chooses. Later, he tricks the two Flashes, Barry Allen and Wally West, into breaking the Force Barrier so that he can access the other forces of the universe trapped behind it: The Sage Force and Strength Force. He then seeks out the Still Force and combines it with the others to create something new—the Forever Force. The Forever Force enables Zoom to manipulate time itself and view any event in time or space.

REVERSE-FLASH

REAL NAME: Daniel West **POWERS:** Connection to Speed Force gives super-speed, reflexes, durability, stamina, agility; advanced healing; time travel; also has metal claws **FIRST APPEARANCE:** *The Flash* Vol 4 #0 (Nov 2012) **SUBSIDIARY CATEGORY:** Accidental

Daniel West, younger brother of Iris, is a troubled kid from a rough background. Following a stint in jail after The Flash foils a robbery he is involved in, Daniel is escaping from the Rogues when he crashes his car into a Speed Force battery housed in a monorail car. As well as acquiring super-speed, Daniel gains the ability to travel in time, and decides to go back to the past and put his life right by killing his abusive father. However, to keep traveling in time, Daniel, taking the identity of the new Reverse-Flash, must drain more Speed Force from others.

DARK FLASH

REAL NAME: Walter West **POWERS:** Connection to Speed Force gives super-speed, reflexes, durability, stamina, agility; advanced healing; dimensional travel **FIRST APPEARANCE:** *The Flash* Vol 2 #150 (Jul 1999) **SUBSIDIARY CATEGORY:** Accidental

Walter West, a.k.a. Dark Flash, is a version of Wally West from an alternate reality in which he is not able to save the life of his true love, Linda Park. He possesses the same powers as his Earth-Zero counterpart, but the trauma he has suffered makes him much harsher in the way he deploys those abilities. In his universe, Walter does not simply defeat the villain Savitar, but learns all he can about the Speed Force from the so-called God of Speed before killing him. When Wally West is believed dead, Walter travels to Wally's reality to take his place, intending to atone for the sins of his past. However, his continuing presence in the "wrong" timeline starts to cause wider problems with the fracturing of reality, and he is forced to leave.

GODSPEED

REAL NAME: August Heart **POWERS:** Connection to Speed Force gives super-speed, reflexes, durability, stamina, agility; advanced healing; speed stealing **FIRST APPEARANCE:** *The Flash: Rebirth* Vol 2 #1 (Aug 2016) **SUBSIDIARY CATEGORY:** Accidental

August Heart, Central City detective and close friend of Barry Allen, is struck by lightning during a Speed Force storm. With his newfound powers, August becomes Godspeed, hell-bent on bringing brutal justice to those who he feels have escaped the reach of the law. He also finds that he can siphon the Speed Force from others to augment his own power, making him—for a time—even faster than Barry Allen. His advanced power means that he can also effectively create temporary clones of himself to be in two places at once, but both this and his ability to steal the Speed Force from other people causes him pain.

FORCES OF THE UNIVERSE:
EMOTIONAL SPECTRUM

GREEN LANTERN

7	Vo
G	
Green Lantern	

REAL NAME: Hal Jordan **POWERS:** Connection to Light of Will gives the ability to create hard-light constructs and force fields, energy blasts, flight, transformation into being of pure will
FIRST APPEARANCE: *Showcase* #22 (Oct 1959)

Hal Jordan is a regular human until he meets a dying alien, Abin Sur, who gives the young test pilot a ring. This gives Hal a connection to a universal force he had no idea existed—the Green Light of Will. Harnessing the power of the ring, Hal becomes a new Green Lantern, a member of an intergalactic organization that protects the innocent. Each Lantern is chosen because of their ability to master fear using their sheer force of willpower, and their rings will only "select" new owners if they fulfill this criterion.

Green Lantern power rings work by channeling the Light of Will from a portable power battery charged from the Central Power Battery on the Green Lanterns' base planet. This energy is then repurposed by the wearer in various ways, encompassing a formidable array of powers. Like all Green Lanterns, Hal Jordan can fly, including through space, and create hard-light constructs for weapons and protection,

While Hal Jordan's pure energy form is very powerful, it causes him to start losing his sense of his true self.

among other things. The constructs can take any shape he chooses—he simply has to will them into being with his mind. It could be said that the potential of a Green Lantern is only limited by that individual's willpower, and Hal Jordan has proven multiple times that his force of will is as great— or greater—than anyone else's.

Hal's personality, and the unusually high level of willpower he demonstrates, leads to him surpassing any previous Green Lantern and accessing new powers. His connection to the Light of Will is so strong that when his power ring is destroyed, he is able to create a replacement through the force of his mind alone. This ring can only be used by Hal or anyone he personally chooses. Later, after accessing the powerful Gauntlet of Krona, Hal gains the ability to turn into a powerful being made only of pure will, but comes to realize that this puts him at risk, both physically and mentally.

EMOTIONAL SPECTRUM

The Green Light of Will that powers Hal Jordan and the Green Lanterns is at the center of the Emotional Electromagnetic Spectrum, a universal energy field that is powered from the emotions of all sentient beings in existence. Green is at the center of the Spectrum, making it the easiest energy to control—those at the outer limits, like the Red Light of Rage and Violet Light of Love, are just as likely to control their users as be mastered by them. In between these are the Orange Light of Avarice, Yellow Light of Fear, Blue Light of Hope, and Indigo Light of Compassion. All colors originate from the White Light of Life, which has the Black Light of Death as its opposite.

Hal comes to either ally with or fight against wielders of the other colors of the Spectrum, and for a time is even himself possessed by the fear entity Parallax, causing great devastation. Yet his great willpower always enables him to overcome personal tragedy and terrible setbacks, and constantly push at the limits of the potential of one of the universe's most powerful energies.

GREEN LANTERN

REAL NAME: John Stewart **POWERS:** Connection to Light of Will through Green Lantern power ring gives the ability to create hard-light constructs and force fields, flight; since "ascension," upper power limits are unknown **FIRST APPEARANCE:** *Green Lantern* Vol 2 #87 (Jan 1972)

John Stewart, a former Marine and architect on Earth, is chosen by the Guardians of the Universe to be a Green Lantern, as they feel he has huge potential to be an asset to the Corps. John does indeed become a great Lantern and rises to the rank of commander of the organization, but that is not the end of his story. He is the only Green Lantern, and the only human at that point, to have also been a Guardian. It is a role that gives him enormous cosmic powers for a time and makes him a valuable "bridge" between Guardians and Lanterns, thanks to his unique perspective. Later, John undergoes an ascension of his powers to seemingly become a higher being, the limits of whose abilities have not yet been reached. He appears to now be linked to The Source from which all life came.

GREEN LANTERN

REAL NAME: Guy Gardner **POWERS:** Connection to Light of Will through Green Lantern power ring gives the ability to create hard-light constructs and force fields, flight **FIRST APPEARANCE:** *Green Lantern* Vol 2 #59 (Mar 1968)

Another Green Lantern from Earth, Guy Gardner has not only been a long-serving member of the Green Lantern Corps, harnessing all the power that the Light of Will bestows, but he has also wielded the power of the Red Light of Rage and become a Red Lantern on several occasions. In fact, Guy is able to call on so much pent up anger and fury from within himself that he defeats the mighty Atrocitus, leader of the Red Lanterns, and takes over that Corps, all as part of an undercover mission for the Green Lanterns. While many of his Green Lantern colleagues might take issue with his hotheadedness and brash attitude, there is no doubting Guy's innate courage—and it is exactly this fearlessness that makes him worthy of the Green Lantern Corps.

GREEN LANTERN

23 **St**
Gk
Green Lantern

REAL NAME: Kyle Rayner **POWERS:** Connection to Light of Will through Green Lantern power ring gives the ability to create hard-light constructs and force fields, flight **FIRST APPEARANCE:** *Green Lantern* Vol 3 #48 (Jan 1994)

Kyle Rayner has been one of the most powerful Lanterns of all time. Starting out as a Green Lantern, he is chosen to wield the rings of all the other colors of the Emotional Spectrum, becoming a White Lantern. This means that for a time he is powered by the Light of Life itself, making him near omnipotent and even capable of changing reality. As well as being able to wield all the powers of the White Light of Life, Kyle can also use any of the other colors of the Spectrum separately if he chooses. Eventually, Kyle has to give up his White Lantern Ring and return to his old comrades as part of the Green Lantern Corps.

GREEN LANTERN

2 **Ba**
Ga
Green Lantern

REAL NAME: Alan Scott **POWERS:** Connection to Light of Will through Starheart power ring gives the ability to create hard-light constructs and force fields, flight, decelerated aging, teleportation, hypnosis, phasing through solid objects **FIRST APPEARANCE:** *All-American Comics* #16 (Jul 1940) **SUBSIDIARY CATEGORY:** Magic

Alan Scott is the first of Earth's Green Lanterns, but the way he accesses his powers differs from those who come after him. He does not use the Green Light of Will from the Central Power Battery, but instead uses the Starheart. This gem is created by the Guardians of the Universe to contain remnants of magical energy that they are trying to purge from the universe, and ends up on Earth encased within a meteor. So while Alan's costume, codename, and powers seem to tie him into the Green Lantern Corps mythos, he is unique, and the Starheart grants him a range of additional powers.

ANCILLARY EXEMPLARS

57 **St**
Bz
Green Lantern
(Simon Baz)

59 **St**
Gj
Green Lantern
(Jessica Cruz)

61 **St**
Sj
Green Lantern
(Jo Mullein)

60 **St**
Tl
Teen Lantern

Earth has produced several Green Lanterns. As well as his Green Lantern powers, **Simon Baz** has developed healing abilities and the "Emerald Sight," which enables visions of the near future. His sometime training partner, **Jessica Cruz**, formerly wielded the power ring of Volthoom, the First Lantern, and since she has anxiety and PTSD, is regularly forced to overcome great fear. **Sojourner "Jo" Mullein** is also given a unique ring, forged by the Guardians to avoid the need to be recharged so that she is not affected by attacks on the Central Power Battery. Keli Quintela, the **Teen Lantern**, not yet a full-fledged Green Lantern, has used her genius to hack into a gauntlet linked to the Central Power Battery.

SINESTRO

REAL NAME: Thaal Sinestro **POWERS:** Connection to Yellow Light of Fear gives the ability to create hard-light constructs and force fields, manipulation of opponents' fear, energy blasts, flight **FIRST APPEARANCE:** *Green Lantern* Vol 2 #7 (Aug 1961) **SUBSIDIARY CATEGORY:** Alien Origins

Sinestro is a master at wielding the Yellow Light of Fear in the Emotional Electromagnetic Spectrum. A former—and some say the greatest—Green Lantern, Sinestro is ejected from the Corps after using his power to become a tyrant on his homeworld of Korugar. Banished to the Antimatter Universe, Sinestro founds a new Corps in his own name, whose rings are forged by the warlike Weaponers of Qward. He uses the Yellow Light of Fear, as that is the one to which the Green Lanterns are most vulnerable. As well as having similar attributes to a Green Lantern power ring, a Sinestro Corps ring can also detect and weaponize the innermost fears of an opponent. Sinestro also builds a Yellow Power Battery on Qward to keep the Yellow power rings charged.

ATROCITUS

REAL NAME: Atros **POWERS:** Super-strength, durability, extremely long-lived; connection to Red Light of Rage gives the ability to create hard-light constructs and force fields, energy blasts, flight, prophecy **FIRST APPEARANCE:** *Green Lantern* Vol 4 #25 (Jan 2008) **SUBSIDIARY CATEGORY:** Magic, Alien Origins

Atrocitus is the leader of the Red Lantern Corps, powered by the Red Light of Rage. Many beings who use the energy of the Emotional Spectrum could be said to inhabit the gray area between science and magic, but the Reds perhaps cleave more to the magical side than most. Their power originates in ancient blood rituals and Atrocitus himself is empowered with demonic energy. He becomes even more powerful by channeling these arcane energies through the rage he feels after his family are killed by Manhunters—lethal androids created by the Guardians of the Universe to eradicate evil across the universe. Fulfilling a prophecy he has seen, Atrocitus kills his demon accomplices and uses their blood to build the Red Power Battery on the corpse planet of Ysmault.

PARALLAX

REAL NAME: Parallax **POWERS:** Energy being that can create hard-light constructs, cause fear; reality manipulation; possession of other entities; shape-changing; immortality **FIRST APPEARANCE:** *Green Lantern* Vol 3 #50 (Mar 1994) **SUBSIDIARY CATEGORY:** Energies

24	Vo
Px	
Parallax	

Parallax is an immortal entity formed from the Yellow Light of Fear. It is parasitic in nature, taking nourishment by inhabiting the body of a living being and feeding on the fear it creates in its host. The emotion of fear can be stoked in virtually any type of creature, so Parallax can become very powerful, although Sinestro manages to enslave the entity to harness its energy for his eponymous Corps. Sinestro even weaponizes the entity to attack individual Green Lanterns by possessing them, with devastating consequences.

While Parallax cannot be killed, it is possible to imprison it, as the Guardians did for many millennia. The entity does not have a fixed form but usually assumes a shape that will instill fear in those who see it, often a giant, monstrous, buglike creature.

SORANIK NATU

REAL NAME: Soranik Natu **POWERS:** Connection to Yellow Light of Fear gives the ability to create hard-light constructs and force fields, manipulation of opponents' fear, energy blasts, flight **FIRST APPEARANCE:** *Green Lantern Corps: Recharge* #1 (Nov 2005) **SUBSIDIARY CATEGORY:** Alien Origins

30	Vo
Sk	
Soranik Natu	

It could be said that being a ring-wielder is in Soranik Natu's genes. She is the niece of Abin Sur, the Green Lantern who bequeaths his ring to Hal Jordan, and the daughter of Sinestro. Like her father, Soranik first becomes a Green Lantern and serves with distinction, but later she joins the Sinestro Corps. When Sinestro apparently dies, Soranik becomes the Corps leader, forging an unlikely alliance with the Green Lanterns until she discovers that they are responsible for the death of her future son. A furious Soranik prepares for battle, but she discovers that the Green Lanterns have implanted a failsafe in the Yellow Power Battery that overrides her ring. With the connection to her power source gone, Soranik leads her Corps to New Korugar to start from scratch.

GREEN LANTERN CORPS

8	Ba
Gc	
Green Lantern Corps	

REAL NAME: Various **POWERS:** Connection to Light of Will through Green Lantern power ring gives the ability to create hard-light constructs and force fields, flight, super-strength, survival in space conditions **FIRST APPEARANCE:** *Showcase* #22 (Oct 1959)

The Green Lantern Corps are created by the Guardians of the Universe to maintain order and keep chaos at bay. Originally, the Corps is organized by having one Green Lantern patrol each of 3,600 space sectors, although later they operate in pairs, necessitating a regular roster of 7,200 Lanterns. Each space sector is wedge-shaped and points at the Green Lantern base planet of Oa, so that Lanterns are still within their sector when on Oa.

Bearers of a Green Lantern power ring are selected for their great courage, which manifests itself as willpower—the mindset to overcome fear. Some members have a ring passed on to them by an existing Corpsman, while others are chosen by the ring itself—when a Green Lantern dies in service, their ring independently seeks out a suitable replacement. Each new Green Lantern is summoned to Oa to undergo training, usually from the tough but fair Kilowog, who makes sure all the "poozers" under his command are prepared for their new life of bringing justice to their assigned space sector.

CODE OF THE CORPS

Kept at the home planet of the Green Lantern Corps is the Book of Oa, at once a history of the Green Lantern Corps and a rule book for them to follow. The Book contains a record of the names and deeds of all the greatest Green Lanterns, whose courage serves to inspire those who come after them. As well as Kilowog and Earth's Green Lanterns, other notable Corps members include Salaak, who has been Keeper of the Book of Oa; Tomar-Re, who tried and failed to save Krypton before dying in service; Graxosian and youngest-ever Green Lantern Arisia

Some members of the Green Lantern Corps are beings almost beyond human understanding, like Dkrtzy RRR, a sentient mathematical equation denoting the formula for willpower.

Rrab; powerful Daxamite Sodam Yat; and sentient planet Mogo, who for a time serves as homeworld for the Corps, and has often been its sanctuary and protector. However, the deeds and laws contained in this most sacred of texts are written in a language only the Guardians can understand, and Lanterns are only permitted to see certain parts of it.

Each Green Lantern channels the Green Light of Will from Oa's Central Power Battery, via small personal Batteries, to their power rings. The concept of the Central Power Battery is billions of years old, and is a testament to the superior science of the Guardians. The Battery acts as a reservoir for the willpower energy of all the sentient beings of the universe.

The construction of the rings allows them to siphon energy from the Battery, while the user's willpower and imagination can then form the energy into hard-light constructs. Hard light is light made into a solid form, which can then be used to real effect—Green Lantern constructs are not illusions to distract, but tools and weapons that can be used as needed. The science of channeling emotional energy in this way is ancient yet incredibly advanced, almost to the point of seeming magic-adjacent to less evolved beings than the Guardians of the Universe.

GUARDIANS OF THE UNIVERSE

REAL NAME: Various **POWERS:** Can absorb and project various forms of energy to create constructs; immortality; telepathy; telekinesis; flight; time travel **FIRST APPEARANCE:** *Green Lantern* Vol 2 #1 (Aug 1960) **SUBSIDIARY CATEGORY:** Alien Origins, Genius Intelligence

11   St

Gd

Guardians of
the Universe

Originally from the planet Maltus, the Guardians of the Universe are among the most ancient species in existence—living reservoirs of cosmic energy. They seek to bring order to all creation and to stamp out chaos, and to achieve this they create the Green Lantern Corps as an interstellar peacekeeping force. The Guardians are so long-lived as to be essentially immortal; they pursue their agendas with a characteristic lack of emotion. Usually appearing as small humanoids with blue skin, in fact they only assume this physical form to put "younger species" at ease in their presence. To them, matter and energy are the same thing, as evidenced by their invention of the Central Power Battery to tap into the universal energy of willpower.

KRONA

REAL NAME: Krona **POWERS:** Can absorb and project various forms of energy to create constructs; immortality; telepathy; telekinesis; flight; time travel **FIRST APPEARANCE:** *Green Lantern* Vol 2 #40 (Oct 1965) **SUBSIDIARY CATEGORY:** Alien Origins, Genius Intelligence

15   Vo

Ka

Krona

Krona is a Guardian of the Universe who is markedly different from his peers, believing that his kind should allow themselves to feel emotions. A genius scientist and seeker of knowledge, he is thought to have come up with the idea for harnessing the energy of willpower and storing it in a battery. However, Krona's curiosity has dire and devastating consequences when he builds a machine to witness the beginning of the universe. His actions not only result in shortening the life of the universe by a billion years but also triggers the formation of the Multiverse. Krona's transgression also causes the total destruction of space sector 666, which leads to the formation of the Green Lantern Corps, and Krona's own banishment in an energy form by the other Guardians.

VOLTHOOM

REAL NAME: Volthoom **POWERS:** Connection to entire Emotional Spectrum enables energy manipulation, construct creation, flight, immortality, regeneration **FIRST APPEARANCE:** *Green Lantern Annual* Vol 5 #1 (Oct 2012) **SUBSIDIARY CATEGORY:** Genius Intelligence, Alternate Earths

Volthoom is a scientist on Earth-15, who, together with his mother, discovers the Emotional Spectrum and invents a "travel lantern," a device for traversing the Multiverse. The lantern can move in three ways: through distance, through time, and between universes.

When Volthoom's Earth is destroyed, he escapes at the last moment with the lantern and goes in search of a way to save his world. While traveling through time and realities, he introduces the power of the Spectrum to those he meets. On Earth-Three he creates the Ring of Volthoom, later used by the evil Crime Syndicate before being passed on to Green Lantern Jessica Cruz.

Eventually he comes to the home of the Guardians of the Universe, where he works alongside them to harness the power of the Emotional Spectrum. At the same time, a power ring manifests apparently out of nowhere, and Volthoom is the first entity to wear one. He volunteers as a guinea pig when the detached emotions of the Guardians are implanted into his chest, but this direct connection to the emotional spectrum overloads his mind.

ANCILLARY EXEMPLARS

While the names of many of the Guardians of the Universe remain unknown to most, a few have allowed their true names to become widely known. These few tend to be those who retain traces of emotions, such as **Ganthet**, who was banished from the Guardians for this reason and went on to found the Blue Lantern Corps, wielders of the Light of Hope. Joining him in these endeavors is his fellow Guardian **Sayd**, and over time the pair develop feelings of love for each other. Another named Guardian is **Scar**, although her moniker is more of a nickname, gained after she is badly wounded in a conflict with the Anti-Monitor. This is a momentous injury, as it brings Scar into contact with the Black and causes her to bring about the Blackest Night, when the Black Lantern Corps are unleashed upon the universe.

STAR SAPPHIRES

REAL NAME: Various **POWERS:** Connection to the Violet Light of Love gives the ability to create constructs and force fields, flight, healing, teleportation to anywhere love is threatened **FIRST APPEARANCE:** *All-Flash* Vol 1 #32 (Jan 1948)

When the Guardians of the Universe choose to purge their emotions, a breakaway group of females rejects this course of action and leaves to forge their own path. They become known as the Zamarons, and create a band of warriors called the Star Sapphires to wield the extremely powerful—although often volatile—Violet Light of Love. At first each of them channels energy through a gem, but these prove very difficult to control, so later the Zamarons fashion a Power Battery and rings like the Green Lantern Corps. One of the most formidable Star Sapphires ever to wield the Violet power ring is Earth's Carol Ferris.

LARFLEEZE

REAL NAME: Larfleeze **POWERS:** Connection to Orange Light of Avarice gives the ability to create constructs and force fields, flight, absorption of other ring-wielders' constructs **FIRST APPEARANCE:** *Green Lantern* Vol 4 #25 (Jan 2008) **SUBSIDIARY CATEGORY:** Alien Origins

Larfleeze is a Sh'pilkuzzian, an extremely hardy and long-lived species. After stealing a map that leads him to the world of Okaara,

he discovers the Orange Light of Avarice. Its power captures him completely, taking over his mind so that all he wants is to possess it. The Light gives Larfleeze a power ring, and, after killing his companions so he does not have to share it, he becomes the sole representative of the Orange Lantern Corps, Agent Orange. After possessing the Light for many years, Larfleeze no longer needs to charge his ring like other Lanterns, as he has become an organic battery for the orange energy.

SAINT WALKER

REAL NAME: Bro'Dee Walker **POWERS:** Connection to Blue Light of Hope gives the ability to create constructs and force fields, healing **FIRST APPEARANCE:** *Green Lantern* Vol 4 #25 (Jan 2008) **SUBSIDIARY CATEGORY:** Alien Origins

Saint Walker wields the Blue Light of Hope for the Blue Lantern Corps, created by breakaway Guardians to help stand against the threat of the Black Lantern Corps. While Saint Walker appears quiet and unassuming, his power should not be underestimated— he once saved a planet by reducing the age of the dying star it orbited. The Blue Light also has a profound effect on Green Lanterns, considerably increasing the power held within their rings. Saint Walker's power ring also enables him to use extraordinary healing powers on others, even to the extent of regenerating lost body parts. His power of hope is so strong that he doesn't lose it even when he is the sole surviving member of his Corps.

INDIGO-1

REAL NAME: Iroque **POWERS:** Connection to Indigo Light of Compassion gives the ability to create constructs and force fields, flight, teleportation **FIRST APPEARANCE:** *Green Lantern* Vol 4 #25 (Jan 2008)

Indigo-1 is the leader and first member of the Indigo Tribe, a Corps based on the planet Nok. The Indigo Light is discovered by Green Lantern Abin Sur and Nok native Natromo, and they realize that it has the power to force even the most hardened criminals and sociopaths to feel remorse for their actions. Abin Sur chooses Iroque to be the Indigo Tribe leader, known as Indigo-1, as she is responsible for killing his daughter. The Indigo Tribe then recruits some of the worst beings in the universe, who are essentially brainwashed by their rings into feeling compassion. The Indigos are able to instantly teleport anywhere in the universe, and also channel the power of other ring-wielders if they are close by.

NEKRON

REAL NAME: Nekron **POWERS:** Killing touch; strength increase from killing; immortality; fires dark energy **FIRST APPEARANCE:** *Tales of the Green Lantern Corps* #2 (Jun 1981) **SUBSIDIARY CATEGORY:** Higher Powers

Nekron is the Lord of the Unliving and the leader of the Black Lantern Corps, an army he creates by using Black Lantern power rings to reanimate the dead. Wearers of these rings retain all the memories of their lives and even their powers, but have no soul. Nekron himself has no need of a power ring as he is an immensely powerful being who is believed to have existed since before life itself, drawing his strength from the void. While his powers are almost beyond comprehension, Nekron is unable to pass into the universe from his realm without some kind of link or avatar.

UMBRAX

REAL NAME: Umbrax **POWERS:** Increases strength by tapping into negative emotions of worlds within its reach; interstellar travel; energy manipulation; light control **FIRST APPEARANCE:** *Justice League* Vol 4 #3 (Sep 2018)

Umbrax is the guiding force of the Invisible Spectrum, which manifests in the form of Ultraviolet energy. Unlike the Emotional Spectrum, the Light of the Invisible Spectrum controls the being to which it is connected, not the other way around. Umbrax is no normal entity, but a sentient black sun at the heart of a living phantom galaxy. This "island" galaxy moves through space searching for planets that exhibit strong self-destructive emotions, like shame and hate, and then pulls them into its orbit. Here they are transformed into sentient entities of a sort, and all their inhabitants join Umbrax's Lantern Corps. Umbrax even infiltrates and infects the primal energies of a planet, like the Red and the Green, so that all life is reduced to its most savage instincts.

AQUAMAN

5   **St**

A

Aquaman

REAL NAME: Arthur Curry **POWERS:** Super-strength, speed, reflexes, durability, stamina; senses; marine telepathy; amphibious
FIRST APPEARANCE: *Adventure Comics* #250 (May 1959)
SUBSIDIARY CATEGORY: Magical, Metagenetic Manifestation

Arthur Curry, a.k.a. Aquaman, is arguably the most remarkable biological specimen on Earth. He is a hybrid, born from a human father and a mother from Atlantis, a city that has existed beneath the sea for thousands of years. Rather than being a diluted version of each aspect of his heritage, Aquaman's hybrid genetics seem to make him exceptional both on land and in the ocean. He is essentially an amphibian, able to survive in either environment, and his strength and durability levels are far in excess of a regular human or Atlantean. His swimming speeds are unparalleled among both, and can reach supersonic levels.

Atlanteans are of the species *Homo magi*, a branch of humankind commonly associated with the practice of magic. This enables them to survive as a species when their entire kingdom is submerged, as they have developed a unique fusion of magic and technology that makes them an extremely advanced civilization. Following rapid evolution, Atlanteans have exceptionally

When Aquaman's Life Force is removed, it severs his connection to the ocean. Like all primordial universal forces, the Life Force has a "hidden" opposite—the Tear of Extinction.

advanced senses, can breathe underwater, and are durable enough to survive the pressures of the deep sea. The hereditary trait of being able to wield and resist magic is less common, and usually found in members of Atlantis' royal family. Since Arthur's mother Atlanna was a princess of Atlantis, he has inherited this affinity with magic through her.

LIFE FORCE

An even rarer power is Aquaman's telepathic link to other living creatures, especially those that live in the ocean. Fish are early ancestors of all life on Earth, and as such have a primal instinct to work together to evolve and survive. Arthur is able to tap into that connection and use it to will other creatures to help him. This astonishing ability comes from Arthur's link to the Life Force, which joins all living creatures, right down to their souls. While this universal energy is present in all beings, it is strongest in those that live in the ocean, the font of all life.

Through his super-heroic career, Aquaman sometimes uses weapons to enhance or focus his existing powers. These are not regular weapons but mystical artifacts befitting a scion of the royal house of Atlantis, like the Trident of Neptune and the Trident of Poseidon. In fact, Aquaman has met and been personally blessed by the sea god Poseidon with a range of extra powers channeled through the Trident, including weather control, power over water, and flight.

A man of two worlds, Aquaman tries to do his best for both, attempting to heal the rift between Atlanteans and the surface-dwellers, and reduce prejudice among his people under the sea, while also attempting to protect the oceans from the harmful actions of those above it. As a founding member of the Justice League, he brings a unique set of skills that are drawn both straight from his physiology and from one of the primordial Forces of the Universe.

MERA

REAL NAME: Mera **POWERS:** Super-strength, speed, reflexes, durability, stamina; senses; amphibious; aquakinesis **FIRST APPEARANCE:** *Aquaman* Vol 1 #11 (Oct 1963) **SUBSIDIARY CATEGORY:** Metagenetic Manifestation

Mera is from the Secret Kingdom of Exiles, Xebel, a realm of Atlanteans that split from Atlantis millennia ago. Xebel resents the way that Atlantis holds itself separate from them, and raises its people to be a fierce warrior race, subsisting on the shipwrecks that fall into their world from above. These shipwrecks gradually build an unnatural reef of wreckage that Xebellians call "The Strand," where warriors like Mera train, and ritual combats are held to settle disputes. Xebel is cut off from Atlantis and the other underwater kingdoms by a solid wall of water, that only someone with aquakinetic abilities can penetrate.

POWER OF WATER

As a member of the royal house of Xebel, Mera has all the usual attributes common to Atlanteans—such as super-speed in the water, an amphibious nature, and enhanced senses—but she is also capable of aquakinesis. Mera can control the water molecules around her, shaping them into constructs for her use, like weapons, shields, or simply a platform to lift her above the surface of the water. She can even create a "water form" of her own body to do battle by proxy, although this is very draining for her. The "hard water" that she creates can be made into bullets solid enough to kill, however, Mera is more merciful than many of her Xebellian brethren and favors nonlethal combat. Trained from childhood to use her power as well as more conventional forms of fighting, Mera is said to be the most powerful aquakinetic ever recorded. This ability also helps boost her speed in the water, enabling her to reach swimming speeds even in excess of Aquaman's.

When Mera uses the full force of her aquakinetic powers, a luminescent glow is visible close to her hands.

AQUALAD

REAL NAME: Jackson Hyde **POWERS:** Super-strength, speed, reflexes, durability, stamina; senses; amphibious; aquakinesis; electrokinesis **FIRST APPEARANCE:** *Brightest Day* #4 (Aug 2010) **SUBSIDIARY CATEGORY:** Energies: Electrical

Like Arthur Curry (Aquaman), Jackson Hyde is an Atlantean-human hybrid. Unlike Arthur, Jackson's Atlantean heritage is Xebellian, and his human heritage is from a super-villain—his father is Black Manta. From his Xebellian mother, Jackson inherits aquakinesis, the ability to control water molecules and shape them into hard-water constructs. Jackson also has an additional power that no other Atlantean shares: electrokinesis. He can emit bioelectricity from his body in the form of blasts, or even channel it through his water constructs, which can have a very dramatic effect. This is because natural water, especially salt water, is an excellent conductor of electricity due to its high mineral content. Jackson works hard to step out of his father's shadow and use his impressive power set for good.

TEMPEST

REAL NAME: Garth **POWERS:** Super-strength, speed, reflexes, durability, stamina; senses; amphibious; marine telepathy; magic **FIRST APPEARANCE:** *Adventure Comics* Vol 1 #269 (Feb 1960) **SUBSIDIARY CATEGORY:** Magical, Metagenetic Manifestation

Garth is an Atlantean, skilled in that civilization's ancient magic. He learns the craft at the Silent School in Atlantis, but abandons using it after a tragic accident kills one of his classmates. He uses his natural physical Atlantean advantages as one of The Titans team, occasionally relaxing his "no magic" rule when the situation is critical. Atlantean sorcery manifests as purple energy that Garth can fire from his hands or eyes. His eyes are purple in color, something that marks him as a magical being and causes him to be feared or shunned by some in Atlantean society. Purple eyes are believed to be the genetic marker for someone descended from ancient sorcerers.

OCEAN MASTER

REAL NAME: Orm Marius **POWERS:** Super-strength, speed, reflexes, durability, stamina, senses; amphibious; enchanted trident gives control of weather **FIRST APPEARANCE:** *Aquaman* Vol 1 #29 (Oct 1966) **SUBSIDIARY CATEGORY:** Metagenetic Manifestation

Orm Marius is the Atlantean half-brother of Aquaman (Arthur Curry), who believes that his "pure" Atlantean blood makes him superior to Arthur, and the better choice to rule Atlantis. As an Atlantean of noble birth, his natural abilities—like strength and durability—are certainly in excess of the norm for Atlantis, and his attitude toward his rights and contempt for surface-dwellers frequently brings him into conflict with Aquaman and his allies, including the Justice League. Orm also wields a trident that grants him additional advantages— the power to channel the wrath of storms, summon hurricanes and tsunamis, or draw lightning down onto his opponents. The trident also enables Orm to control the magnetic field and move metal objects in his vicinity.

TULA

REAL NAME: Tula Marius **POWERS:** Super-strength, speed, reflexes, durability, stamina, senses; amphibious **FIRST APPEARANCE:** *Aquaman* Vol 1 #33 (May 1967) **SUBSIDIARY CATEGORY:** Metagenetic Manifestation

Tula Marius is the half-sister of Orm Marius, a.k.a. Ocean Master—they have the same father. Tula is a full-blooded Atlantean, so she is naturally capable of metahuman feats such as super-speed in the water, plus she possesses enhanced senses and the ability to survive in extreme oceanic conditions. As she is not of the direct royal line like Orm or Arthur Curry, Tula's abilities are lesser; however, she is a skilled fighter, raised and trained to join her half-brother in the Drift, an elite yet covert military unit of Atlantis. Tula's star rises higher when she is named Regent of Atlantis by her ally Aquaman, reigning in his stead.

CORUM RATH

REAL NAME: Corum Rath **POWERS:** Super-strength, speed, reflexes, durability, stamina, senses; amphibious; various magical enhancements **FIRST APPEARANCE:** *Aquaman: Rebirth* #1 (Aug 2016) **SUBSIDIARY CATEGORY:** Magical

Atlantis is divided geographically into layers called "trides," with the ninth of these being the lowest in both senses. This slum is where Corum Rath is born and raised, harboring a great resentment that leads him to foment a terrorist uprising and eventually seize the throne itself for a time. He is aided in this enterprise by his use of ancient Atlantean magicks, which give him the edge over his rivals. Unlike many, who distrust and fear magic, Corum believes it is the foundation on which Atlantis is built and will help the civilization to one day take its rightful place ruling both the oceans and the surface world. However, Corum's dependence on magic soon leads to the loss of his sanity.

NEREUS

38	Vo
Ne	
Nereus	

REAL NAME: Nereus **POWERS:** Super-strength, speed, reflexes, durability, stamina, senses; amphibious; aquakinetics **FIRST APPEARANCE:** *Aquaman* Vol 7 #19 (Jun 2013)

Nereus is a leading warlord of Xebel, the breakaway Atlantean kingdom beneath what surface-dwellers call the Bermuda Triangle. As one of the Xebellian elite, he has the power of aquakinetics, able to manipulate water into constructs or to strike his opponents. Nereus has not always had this ability—he had expected to receive it when he married Mera, which ultimately does not happen—but after taking the throne of Xebel, he accesses the secrets of mastering water. This suggests that aquakinetics is an acquired skill rather than a genetic inheritance, although possibly one that can only be learned by someone of Atlantean heritage.

DOLPHIN

19	St
Do	
Dolphin	

REAL NAME: Dolphin **POWERS:** Super-strength, speed, reflexes, durability, stamina, senses; amphibious; bioluminescent powers; claws; camouflage **FIRST APPEARANCE:** *Showcase* Vol 1 #79 (Dec 1968) **SUBSIDIARY CATEGORY:** Metagenetic Manifestation

Dolphin is an example of what the Atlanteans call "sea-changed"— an Atlantean mutated by exposure to the ocean. She has webbed, clawed hands, and scaly limbs. Often shunned by Atlanteans, these beings can develop additional powers to that of normal Atlanteans. In Dolphin's case, she possesses bioluminescence, which allows her to emit a pulse of extremely bright light, strong enough to induce seizures in those close by. Found in various marine creatures, this phenomenon is caused by a chemical reaction within the body. Dolphin is mute, but she can use her bioluminescence to draw messages in the air.

ANCILLARY EXEMPLARS

47	Vo
An	
Atlanna	

62	St
Ac	
Andy Curry	

48	St
Nv	
Nuidis Vulko	

58	St
Mu	
Murk	

Aquaman's family also have special abilities: Like her son Arthur, **Queen Atlanna** of Atlantis has a telepathic link to marine life. Aquaman's daughter with Mera, Princess Andrina, a.k.a. **Andy Curry**, has inherited her mother's ability to control water, a signature ability of the Xebellian royal family. A loyal advisor to the royal family, **Nuidis Vulko** has all the regular Atlantean powers but his vast knowledge of the realm has been indispensable to multiple rulers. The top military commander in Atlantis is **Murk**, who also has no extra powers but is made more formidable thanks to the blade that has replaced his lost right arm.

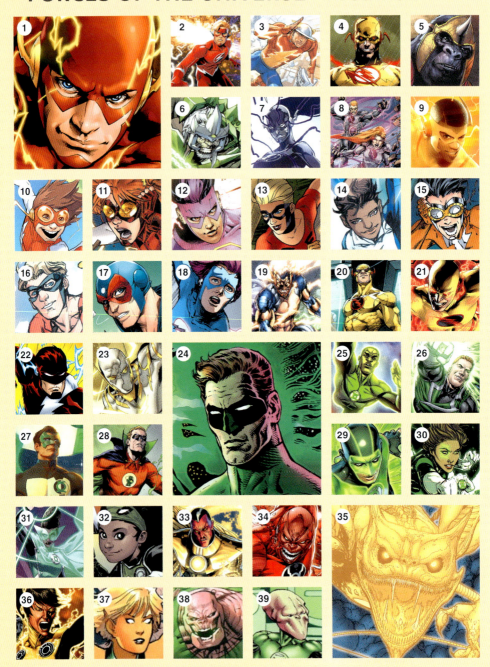

EARTH ELEMENTS

Some beings take their abilities from the elements found in nature, including the potent divine metals, the webs of life connecting all living organisms, and energy in all its forms.

Me METALS

There are five divine metals that separately confer great powers, and together can open a portal to the Dark Multiverse.

23 St **Cy** Cyborg	1 St **H** Hawkman	2 St **Hg** Hawkgirl	7 Ba **Ml** Metal Men	15 Vo **Ra** Rā's al Ghūl	24 Vo **Dk** Deathstroke	37 St **Tm** The Signal
38 St **Sd** Sideways	14 Vo **Ti** Talia al Ghūl	36 Ba **Ow** Talons	40 Tx **Tz** Task Force Z			

Na NATURAL WORLD

Some beings have a special bond with the Green or the Red, the webs linking plant and animal life respectively.

16 St **Sw** Swamp Thing (Alec Holland)	13 Tx **Iv** Poison Ivy	4 Vo **C** The Cheetah	12 St **Ai** Animal Man	27 St **Mk** Animal Girl	25 St **Vx** Vixen	9 Tx **Fc** Floronic Man
6 St **Cp** Detective Chimp	39 St **Lk** Swamp Thing (Levi Kamei)	19 St **Oh** Black Orchid	47 Ba **Pt** Parliament of Trees	52 Ba **Lm** Parliament of Limbs	53 Tx **Pa** Parliament of Decay	5 Vo **So** Solomon Grundy
31 Vo **Ks** King Shark	17 Tx **Aa** Anton Arcane	18 Tx **Ab** Abby Arcane	50 Vo **Oa** Orca	41 Vo **Bh** Black Hand	45 Vo **Rd** Brother Blood	

ENERGIES—NUCLEAR/RADIOACTIVE

While nuclear energy can be powerful, toxic, or both, it can also have a transformative effect on a few humans.

22 Co	26 Co	21 St	10 St	43 Vo	48 Vo	42 Co
Fi	**Ca**	**Bb**	**Nm**	**Mp**	**Rj**	**Po**
Firestorm	Captain Atom	Bumblebee	Negative Man	Multiplex	Parasite	Doctor Phosphorus

ENERGIES—LIGHT

Some individuals have the ability to convert the light that emanates all around us into incredible abilities.

29 Re	3 St	8 Co	33 Co
Ry	**Hp**	**Dl**	**Su**
Ray (Raymond Terrill)	Ray (Langford "Happy" Terrill)	Doctor Light	Solaris

ENERGIES—COSMIC

In space there is a near limitless reserve of interstellar energies for those able or willing to tap into it.

28 St	30 Vo	11 Co	34 Vo
Wp	**Cs**	**He**	**Ix**
Starman (William Payton)	Cyborg Superman	Heat Wave	Imperiex

ENERGIES—ELECTRICAL

Electric energy has long fascinated human scientists, and some have merged it with their own bodies.

20 Ba	35 St	32 St	51 Co	46 Co	44 Co	49 St
Bl	**Lg**	**Jn**	**Lw**	**Db**	**El**	**Vh**
Black Lightning	Lightning	Jenny Sparks	Livewire	Deathbolt	Electrocutioner	Static

CYBORG

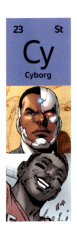

23   St

Cy

Cyborg

REAL NAME: Victor Stone **POWERS:** Super-strength, stamina, durability, senses; flight; mechanokinesis; technology communication; Boom Tube technology **FIRST APPEARANCE:** *DC Comics Presents* Vol 1 #26 (Oct 1980) **SUBSIDIARY CATEGORY:** Constructed Beings, Genius Intelligence

Victor Stone's life changes forever when he is caught in an explosion at S.T.A.R. Labs, the workplace of his father, Silas. In a critical condition, Victor is patched up by his scientist dad using a variety of cutting-edge technological gadgets he has in his lab. Even his bones are strengthened with molybdenum-steel. At the end of the extensive procedure, Victor becomes Cyborg, a being who is part man, part machine. While it is difficult for Victor to come to terms with this complete overhaul of his physiology, he is eventually able to see the advantages of his new body.

HUMAN: UPGRADED

Cyborg's most obvious new feature is his armor, made from depleted Promethium, an alloy that is near-unbreakable.

Cyborg is mechanokinetic—he can shape the robotic parts of his body into different tools in response to different mission requirements.

Due to his injuries, this armor is not to be removed—it provides constant protection for the remaining organic parts of his body, as well as for the advanced tech components inside. This includes an extensive computer system containing a database on all known metahumans, as well as all medical knowledge in the Multiverse.

As Victor's brain is still "merely" human, albeit one with genius-level intelligence, there is the risk that he will become overwhelmed with the sheer amount of data that he can process. With the help of Batman, he installs a filtering system so that only the most important facts are presented to his conscious mind at any one time.

In the operation to save his son's life, Silas Stone injected Victor with nanites, microscopic robots that can carry out a variety of functions within the body, such as enhancing all senses to superhuman levels (including a mechanical infrared-sensing eye to replace the eye he loses in the accident) and repairing and upgrading both organic and nonorganic parts. This means that Cyborg is always in peak condition, including maintaining his tech components at cutting-edge levels. However, his high level of computerization also makes him vulnerable to extremely sophisticated hacking.

As Apokolyptian Mother Box technology is involved in the explosion that led to Cyborg's creation, he has the built-in ability to create Boom Tubes for interdimensional travel. However, he tries to avoid using this function, as one in a thousand Boom Tube journeys will land him on Apokolips. Instead, his new body offers a range of other ways to travel—jump jets and rocket boosters enable flight, while force fields and other tech protect him from extreme environments like space and the deep ocean. This link to the Mother Box also means a connection to Element X, or Tenth Metal, which powers it. Tenth Metal is the purest form of creation, and anyone linked to it has advanced powers and cosmic awareness. Cyborg's main weapon is the "white noise cannon" that forms his entire lower arm, which releases powerful sonic blasts that can actually disintegrate opponents if he chooses to. Victor also has the ability to re-form the components of his body to create alternative weapons and tools to suit different situations.

Cyborg is the technological marvel that brings an extra dimension to teams like the Justice League and The Titans that no other hero can. It is not just his gadgetry that makes him a valued teammate, but his humanity, which still shines through all the high-tech embellishments. Victor's friendship and loyalty are just as important to his colleagues as his weaponry and AI.

HAWKMAN

REAL NAME: Carter Hall **POWERS:** Connection to Nth Metal gives super-strength and durability, flight, healing, decelerated aging, reincarnation **FIRST APPEARANCE:** *Flash Comics* Vol 1 #1 (Jan 1940) **SUBSIDIARY CATEGORY:** Alien Origins, Divine

Hawkman is one of the most complex beings in the Multiverse. Originally a mass-murdering alien called Ktar Deathbringer, on his own death he is given the opportunity by godlike entity The Presence to atone for his sins by saving as many lives as he has ended. Since this constitutes a very large number, Ktar is given the gift—or some might say curse—of reincarnation. He lives thousands of lives across space and time, trying to make up for his lethal past. He also has a special connection with the planet Thanagar, from which Nth Metal is derived. This powerful substance possesses a range of useful attributes that when forged into clothing or weapons can enable its wielders to fly, increases their strength, and provides them with accelerated healing.

HAWKGIRL

REAL NAME: Kendra Saunders **POWERS:** Connection to Nth Metal gives super-strength and durability, flight, healing, decelerated aging, reincarnation **FIRST APPEARANCE:** *Flash Comics* Vol 1 #1 (Jan 1940) **SUBSIDIARY CATEGORY:** Divine

Hawkgirl is the spirit of a Herald of The Presence. When she observes good in the murderous Ktar (later Hawkman), she is cursed to reincarnate repeatedly with him as he atones for all the lives he took in his first existence. Like him, Hawkgirl gains special powers from Nth Metal, a "psychic metal" that reacts to emotions. Also like Hawkman, she has a vast knowledge of history and fighting techniques accrued over time through her many lives. At one point, the extradimensional Perpetua splits Hawkgirl's soul in two, hoping to diminish her power as she is fated to oppose her. This intervention leads to the simultaneous existence of two incarnations of Hawkgirl, in the personas of Kendra Saunders of Earth and Shayera Hol, or Hawkwoman of Thanagar.

METAL MEN

REAL NAME: Various **POWERS:** Shape-shifting; various other abilities depending on the nature of the metal **FIRST APPEARANCE:** *Showcase* Vol 1 #37 (Apr 1962) **SUBSIDIARY CATEGORY:** Lab Created

The Metal Men are a very special group of Super Heroes. Each member comprises an AI bonded with a different kind of metal, using a remarkable device called a Responsometer. These cutting-edge gadgets are created by Dr. Will Magnus, an exceptional engineer, who theorized that natural elements could have their own personality traits if they could be channeled. The Responsometer, when placed into a pure metal, animates that metal into a sentient, humanoid being with specific characteristics that relate to their base element. The device then records that being's personality and memories, making it possible to transfer those traits to a new body if the existing one is somehow damaged beyond repair.

MEET THE METALS

The original Metal Men are Gold, Platinum (Tina for short), Tin, Lead, Mercury, and Iron. Each is able to reshape their bodies to suit the situation they encounter, and each has a unique character. Gold is a leader, albeit somewhat arrogant, Tina is loyal, Tin is self-deprecating and uncertain,

Lead is strong but slow, Mercury is volatile and angry, while Iron is tough and always ready for battle.

Following an encounter with Nth Metal Man, who is just like them except that he needs no Responsometer, the Metal Men discover that they have never had true sentience or personalities, but are just echoing shards of Dr. Magnus' personality. After Nth Metal Man fully awakens their Responsometers, the Metal Men experience true awareness and emotions for the first time. However, even after achieving true autonomy, they choose to keep using their powers for good, acting independently of Dr. Magnus and with their own style.

When Dr. Will Magnus' Responsometer is immersed in molten metal, it emits an electric signal that bonds the two together. Every atom of the metal can then be manipulated to form a shape.

RĀ'S AL GHŪL

REAL NAME: Unknown **POWERS:** Immortality; prodigious intellect; martial arts; weaponry **FIRST APPEARANCE:** *Batman* Vol 1 #232 (Jun 1971) **SUBSIDIARY CATEGORY:** Superior Talents, Magical

Rā's al Ghūl, also known as the Demon's Head, is a remarkable human. He has spent many centuries acquiring arguably unequaled knowledge and skills, including multiple languages, various sciences including alchemy, and a wide range of martial arts and fighting techniques. He is an expert with most historical weapons and a formidable one-on-one combat opponent. He has also been able to pick up various mystical skills and has some working understanding of magic and the occult. Although part of his vast intellect reflects the amount of time he has had to learn compared to most humans, Rā's is a naturally gifted thinker and also has a photographic memory.

LAZARUS RISING

The secret to Rā's long life, which amounts to practical immortality, is his knowledge of Lazarus Pits. He first discovers these phenomena while searching for a cure for the prince for whom he was employed as a doctor. The Lazarus Pits contain a usually green liquid of uncertain chemical composition, although it is known that they contain Dionesium. This is a liquid metal that has life-restoring and healing properties, even to the extent of bringing the dead back to life. It is also one of the five metals that—when combined—results in the opening of a portal to the Dark Multiverse.

Exposure to the Lazarus Pits restores a person's physical health, but at a—usually temporary—cost of their sanity. While Rā's understands the Lazarus Pits better than anyone, it is likely that his prolonged use of them over hundreds of years has had a more lasting effect on his mental stability, and has caused him to use his many gifts to further his own ambitions for world domination.

Rā's al Ghūl's knowledge of, and access to, the Lazarus Pits makes him effectively immortal.

DEATHSTROKE

REAL NAME: Slade Wilson **POWERS:** Super-strength, durability, speed, stamina, agility, reflexes, senses; advanced healing factor; decelerated aging **FIRST APPEARANCE:** *New Teen Titans* Vol 1 #2 (Dec 1980) **SUBSIDIARY CATEGORY:** Serum, Metagenetic Manifestation, Superior Talents

Slade "Deathstroke" Wilson is a self-professed Terminator. Not only is he highly trained in the art of combat, including proficiency in a wide range of weaponry, but he is also a metahuman. Slade volunteers for a program called the Advanced Soldier Initiative, where he is injected with a serum that activates a dormant metagene to accelerate the evolution of his brain. This vastly increases his cognitive capacity and also has an effect on the rest of his body, controlled by the brain, granting him a range of superhuman abilities and a powerful healing factor. His aging process is significantly slower than regular humans, and he also possesses a resistance to toxins, making him an extremely difficult opponent to get the better of.

IKONIC

In addition to his enhanced physical attributes, Deathstroke also utilizes the phenomenally advanced Ikon suit. It is made of Promethium, one of the five metals that opens a gateway to the Dark Multiverse. Since it is the volatile, mutagenic version of that alloy, Deathstroke's suit would in fact cause him physical harm if it were not for his advanced healing factor, which enables him to recover from virtually any injury. The suit's properties allow it to absorb the impact of almost any blow or projectile, and it is powered by the kinetic energy generated by Deathstroke as he moves. He has also wielded swords containing Promethium. Deathstroke pushes everything to the limit of its potential, whether that be the metahuman abilities of his body or the performance of his armor and weapons, all in the service of his reputation as the world's deadliest assassin.

Deathstroke lost his right eye after his then wife, Adeline, shot him in anger over his failure to protect their son, Joseph. However, thanks to his increased brain activity he seems to suffer no ill effects in his vision and has claimed to fight better without it.

EARTH ELEMENTS: METALS

THE SIGNAL

REAL NAME: Duke Thomas **POWERS:** Photokinesis; umbrakinesis; healing; prodigious intellect
FIRST APPEARANCE: *Batman* Vol 2 #21 (Aug 2013) **SUBSIDIARY CATEGORY:** Metagenetic
Manifestation, Energies: Light, Genius Intelligence

37	St
Tm	
The Signal	

Unlike the majority of the Batman Family, Duke Thomas is a metahuman. His father is the immortal villain Gnomon, and his mother Elaine is also a metahuman who keeps her powers concealed to protect her family. Duke's metagene is connected to the traces of Nth Metal that flow in his blood. He possesses powers over shadow and light—umbrakinesis and photokinesis—and can make himself invisible by changing the light around him. Duke is also able to see the path of light, and where it has come from, enabling him to effectively see a few minutes into the past in any scenario in which he finds himself. He calls this his "Ghost Vision." He can absorb darkness into himself, or use shadows to move imperceptibly for stealth.

SIDEWAYS

REAL NAME: Derek James **POWERS:** Super-strength, durability, reflexes, agility; instant interdimensional travel through rifts **FIRST APPEARANCE:** *Sideways* Vol 1 #1 (Apr 2018)
SUBSIDIARY CATEGORY: Metagenetic Manifestation

38	St
Sd	
Sideways	

Derek James believes himself to be an ordinary teenager until he falls through a rift into the Dark Multiverse. However, he has always carried traces of Nth Metal in his blood, and when this is exposed to the energies found in the Dark Multiverse, it triggers his latent metagene. The powers that Derek develops in that moment are what enable him to return to his own world, as he now has the ability to create his own rifts in space-time. Through these, he can move between any two points in the Multiverse and beyond. As the hero Sideways, Derek discovers that the solid edges of his rifts mean that they can also be used as shields and even as throwing weapons. Perhaps his most dangerous power, though, is the ability to create his own black holes.

TALIA AL GHŪL

REAL NAME: Talia al Ghūl **POWERS:** Martial arts, weaponry skills; immortality through Lazarus Pits **FIRST APPEARANCE:** *Detective Comics* Vol 1 #411 (May 1971) **SUBSIDIARY CATEGORY:** Superior Talents

Learning from her father Rā's that humans are a curse upon the planet Earth, Talia al Ghūl is raised to be an ecoterrorist just like him. She is taught to wield a wide range of weapons, and trained relentlessly in fighting techniques so that she can stand beside her father in his League of Assassins. Rā's has also indoctrinated Talia with the secrets of the Lazarus Pits and their life-giving metal Dionesium, which grants her functional immortality and the ability to be cured of wounds or disease that would kill other humans. Lazarus Pits can only be used once, so Talia must also learn from Rā's how to live a nomadic life in search of the next pit, usually found where mystical ley lines cross.

TALONS

REAL NAME: Various **POWERS:** Resurrection, healing; trained in martial arts and weaponry **FIRST APPEARANCE:** *Batman* Vol 2 #2 (Dec 2011) **SUBSIDIARY CATEGORY:** Superior Talents

Talons are the ruthless assassins employed by the Court of Owls, a secret organization that has influenced events in Gotham City for centuries. Even if they fall in service of their masters, the Court can reanimate deceased Talons using the highly conductive alloy of silver and copper known as Electrum, one of the metals that combine to open a portal to the Dark Multiverse. A small amount of the alloy is implanted in a tooth of the Talon, gradually leaching into the rest of their body over years. The presence of Electrum in their cells means that they are able to be healed and even resurrected over and over again.

TASK FORCE Z

REAL NAME: Various **POWERS:** Various **FIRST APPEARANCE:** *Detective Comics* Vol 1 #1043 (Nov 2021) **SUBSIDIARY CATEGORY:** Serum

Task Force Z is a government-sponsored organization using undead metahumans for paramilitary operations. The deceased are reanimated using Lazarus Resin, a concentrated substance created from the liquid inside a Lazarus Pit and therefore containing the life-giving metal Dionesium. Subjects given the resin must keep being administered doses of it or they will revert back to a death state again. However, too high a dose can result in loss of sanity— if the subject had been sane to begin with— heightened aggression, and cannibalistic tendencies. The resin also has to be kept away from contact with the living, for their own safety. Project Halperin is set up to run Task Force Z so that doses of Lazarus Resin can be carefully measured and its effects recorded for research purposes. Its ultimate goal is to be able to use the resin for wider military applications, creating an army of unkillable soldiers.

SWAMP THING

16	St
Sw	
Swamp Thing	

REAL NAME: Alec Holland **POWERS:** Connection to the Green gives chlorokinesis—control over plant life; metamorphosis; super-strength **FIRST APPEARANCE:** *House of Secrets* Vol 1 #92 (Jul 1971) **SUBSIDIARY CATEGORY:** Metagenetic Manifestation

Botanist Dr. Alec Holland invents the Bio-Restorative Formula, designed to trigger the growing of plants in the driest regions on the planet. But his interest in plants goes beyond scientific curiosity. He is one of a number of humans born with a special connection to the Green, the elemental force connecting all plant life in the universe. This is not something magical, but a genetic variation that exists within those people. Even among beings such as this, Alec is special, as he is earmarked as a warrior king of the Green, to act as its protector and champion.

When Alec's Louisiana laboratory is destroyed in an explosion, his body is doused in Bio-Restorative Formula and hurled into the swamp. Although his human body is dead, his memories and consciousness—the essence of his self—are imbued into the surrounding plant matter and reborn as a creature made of ambulant vegetation: Swamp Thing. It is not Alec Holland transformed, but a new entity entirely, although it believes itself to be the scientist until a later rebirth reveals the truth.

Scientifically, Swamp Thing's body is a marvel. The matter of which it is made behaves similarly to stem cells in animals, and any part of it is capable of growing any type of plant cell, guided by the will of Swamp Thing himself. This means that he can spawn poisonous plants on his body to use as weapons, grow winglike appendages to fly, and heal himself by growing new plant matter to replace any damaged areas. He can also change his size by growing or shedding vegetation,

Dr. Alec Holland's genius for botany is such that he, with his wife Linda, creates a formula that can enable deserts to be seeded with life-giving plants, even at temperatures of 125°F (52°C).

and even create duplicates of himself. A side effect of this is that Alec Holland is effectively immortal, and can regrow his Swamp Thing body from any plant cell on Earth.

AVATAR OF THE GREEN

Despite this ability to regrow, elemental beings like Swamp Thing do have a natural, albeit usually very long, lifespan. When that comes to an end, their spirits join the Parliament of Trees, the council of plant elementals that selects a new Avatar of the Green as the time comes—when a new Swamp Thing is needed. Alec Holland is selected as that champion at a time when the Green is more threatened than ever before, as the impact of humans on the planetary ecosystem is reaching catastrophic levels. To be at the center of this conflict triggers a different conflict—the one within Swamp Thing himself as he struggles with his identity. Is he still in any sense a human; does he retain some humanity as a result of having Alec Holland's consciousness? Or is he purely of the Green, and must oppose humans as the potential destroyers of Earth? Swamp Thing is a mighty defender of plant life, and can be persuaded sometimes to use his formidable powers to help Super Hero teams with their own missions. However, he is a law unto himself, and his elemental side can be in the ascendancy over his human side, making him unpredictable as an ally.

POISON IVY

REAL NAME: Pamela Isley **POWERS:** Control over plant life; production of toxins and pheromones
FIRST APPEARANCE: *Batman* Vol 1 #181 (Jun 1966) **SUBSIDIARY CATEGORY:** Lab Created,
Genius Intelligence

Pamela Isley is a scientist researching the effect of plant pheromones, chemicals that are released by individuals to trigger responses in others. She is idealistic, and devoted to her mentor, Jason Woodrue. One day, he conducts an experiment on her that fundamentally changes her body, replacing her blood with chlorophyll and her sweat with poison. Pamela is also capable of producing such powerful pheromones that she can make anybody fall in love with her. This is a dangerous state to be in, as Poison Ivy's kiss can be highly toxic—she can produce the deadliest form of plant toxins in her body and secrete them at will.

Following such dramatic changes, Pamela's sense of self is undermined and she lashes out at men, whom she holds responsible for what has happened to her, and at humankind in general, who she blames for the ongoing destruction to the world around her. While her mind erodes, her powers become far stronger, and she realizes she can control plant life on a global scale.

THE GREATER GOOD

Poison Ivy's powers are connected to the Green, the elemental force flowing through all plant life. After the experiment that gave her powers, she is no longer fully human, but her DNA has been altered to make her a plant-human hybrid. Like a plant, she can regrow any damaged or missing body parts, and even has functional immortality due to being able to regenerate through any plant with which she has had contact. Ivy becomes an ecoterrorist, her ambition being to save and protect all plant life on Earth, and if any humans get in her way, she won't hesitate to take drastic action for her greater good.

Poison Ivy's research in hybridization leads to the creation of her "children," rapid-growth plant-human hybrids called Rose, Hazel, and Thorn.

THE CHEETAH

REAL NAME: Barbara Ann Minerva **POWERS:** Super-strength, durability, speed, stamina, agility, reflexes; razor-sharp fangs and claws **FIRST APPEARANCE:** *Wonder Woman* Vol 1 #6 (Sep 1943) **SUBSIDIARY CATEGORY:** Divine

Archaeologist Dr. Barbara Ann Minerva is searching for the true location of the legendary Themyscira when she encounters the plant god Urzkartaga in Africa. The god forces her to become his bride, which involves a ritual that turns her into a human-animal hybrid, The Cheetah.

Barbara is now essentially a demigod, having been divinely empowered. In her form as The Cheetah, she appears as a humanoid version of that big cat, with spotty fur, sharp teeth and claws, and a long tail. She is also more savage than in her human form, and has an insatiable hunger for flesh. She possesses enhanced senses and various superhuman abilities that place her far in advance of the animal she resembles, including, of course, phenomenal super-speed and agility. She is powerful enough to be a formidable enemy, even to Wonder Woman. Formerly a close friend to the Amazon, but also blaming her for her transformation into The Cheetah, Barbara veers between trying to be an ally and being Diana's most persistent nemesis.

CALL OF THE WILD

When Wonder Woman frees her from Urzkartaga, Barbara returns to human form, but the memory of being The Cheetah does not leave her. She still has a dual nature, seemingly making it impossible for her to be truly happy—to be truly herself—in either form. Eventually, she returns in her form as The Cheetah in order to save her friends, and once back in the animalistic mindset, she does not want to become human again. However, Wonder Woman never gives up hope that her old friend can be cured of her feral tendencies.

As The Cheetah, Barbara Ann does not retain any physical imperfections from her human form, like her limp or her need to wear glasses.

ANIMAL MAN

REAL NAME: Buddy Baker **POWERS:** Can commune with the life web and take on characteristics of any animal **FIRST APPEARANCE:** *Strange Adventures* Vol 1 #180 (Sep 1965)

Buddy Baker is Animal Man, the Avatar of the Red, a phenomenon also known as the Morphogenetic Field. The Red is an energy field that contains the spirits of all animals that have ever lived, on Earth and beyond. Buddy is able to tap into this energy and take on the abilities of any animal in the universe, past or present. The full incredible range of natural animal abilities is available to Buddy—flight, deep-ocean survival, proportionate strength and speed, wall-crawling, camouflage, and many more. He can also communicate with and control animals. He is the champion and protector of the elemental force connecting all animal life, but he is not the first choice of the Parliament of Limbs, the council of spirits who choose the Avatar. Buddy is only the interim holder of the role until the next true Avatar—his daughter Maxine—is ready.

ANIMAL GIRL

REAL NAME: Maxine Baker **POWERS:** Connection to the Red gives communication with and control of animals, ability to take on powers of animals, and healing **FIRST APPEARANCE:** *Animal Man* Vol 1 #1 (Sep 1988) **SUBSIDIARY CATEGORY:** Metagenetic Manifestation

Maxine Baker is a pure Avatar of the Red, born to the role. This is in contrast to her father Buddy, who is granted the connection to the Red as an adult on a temporary basis only. Maxine's powers are therefore far stronger than Buddy's, although she is not yet in full control of them as she is still a child. As well as possessing the ability to communicate with and assume the characteristics of all animals that have ever existed by tapping into the Red, or Morphogenetic Field, Maxine can also control animals at a fundamental level. This includes being able to influence their life cycles, and therefore bring them back from the dead. Additionally, she can purge the destructive Rot energy from their bodies, and also use her healing ability on her own body.

VIXEN

REAL NAME: Mari McCabe **POWERS:** Connection to the Red gives powers of any animal, boosted with Tantu Totem **FIRST APPEARANCE:** *Action Comics* Vol 1 #521 (Jul 1981) **SUBSIDIARY CATEGORY:** Divine, Metagenetic Manifestation

Mari McCabe inherits a mystical artifact, the Tantu Totem, which activates her connection to the Red, the web of animal life, and enables her to utilize the attributes of any animal. This fox-shaped amulet comes to her from her mother, but it is originally fashioned by the mischievous spider-god Anansi, who is also Mari's ancestor. She is able to use her powers without the Totem, but they are more limited that way. As the hero Vixen, Mari can select whichever animal powers she feels are most useful at any given moment—for example, the incredible tracking abilities of a bear for investigation work, the strength of an elephant, or the leap of a dolphin. Her mission in life is to protect the innocent, whether they be human or animal.

FLORONIC MAN

REAL NAME: Jason Woodrue **POWERS:** Connection to the Green gives chlorokinesis—control over plant life, metamorphosis, super-strength **FIRST APPEARANCE:** *The Atom* Vol 1 #1 (Jul 1962) **SUBSIDIARY CATEGORY:** Magical

Jason Woodrue, the Floronic Man, is a brilliant but unscrupulous botanist who discovers that it is possible for an ordinary human to become an Avatar of the Green, and engineers a way for himself to gain the position and the powers that go with it. After losing his connection to the Green, the Floronic Man manages to manipulate the Parliament of Flowers, which has bloomed to replace the Parliament of Trees, to regain access to the Green. He achieves this by befriending and then consuming the Parliament of Flowers' chosen champion, the King of Petals, and taking his powers into himself directly. Floronic Man's connection to the Green gives him control of plant life, the capacity to regrow his body and the ability to create plant creatures to do his bidding.

DETECTIVE CHIMP

REAL NAME: Bobo T. Chimpanzee **POWERS:** Immortality; multilingualism; prodigious intellect
FIRST APPEARANCE: *Adventures of Rex the Wonder Dog* Vol 1 #4 (Aug 1952) **SUBSIDIARY**
CATEGORY: Genius Intelligence, Magical, Accidental

Bobo is a naturally intelligent chimpanzee, but his intellect is boosted to phenomenal levels when he chances upon the Fountain of Youth and drinks from it. He becomes Detective Chimp, possessing one of the finest minds on Earth, with a particular flair for investigation, and of course he is restored to youth and no longer ages. Another unexpected side effect on Bobo's improved brain is that he now understands all other animal languages, including human, and can speak them as well. This makes him a remarkable creature by any standards, presenting with the basic biology of a regular chimpanzee but in reality a polyglot genius who can talk to humans.

OBLIVION

Bobo's mind is so active that he falls into the habit of trying to block out or slow down his thoughts. He becomes a regular at the Oblivion Bar, a drinking den and meeting point hidden in a pocket dimension of magic, and a theoretically safe space for the more weird and wonderful residents of the Multiverse. It is only accessible to those with a connection to magic, which Bobo has thanks to the Fountain of Youth. The bar is run by Bobo's good friend Nightmaster, but when he is killed during the invasion of the Dark Multiverse, Detective Chimp finds himself in charge of both the bar and Nightmaster's mystical weapon, the Sword of Night. The blade can open portals to a magical realm called Myrra of which Nightmaster is protector. The troubled but brilliant chimp struggles with the grief and responsibility, but finds a place on the magical Super Hero team Justice League Dark.

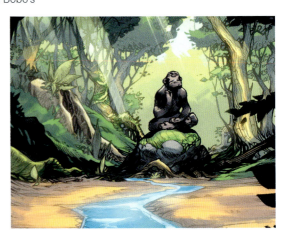

Former circus animal Bobo gains immortality and genius intelligence after discovering the Fountain of Youth, which also gives him a link to the world of magic.

SWAMP THING

39	St
Lk	
Swamp Thing	

REAL NAME: Levi Kamei **POWERS:** Connection to the Green gives chlorokinesis—control over plant life, metamorphosis, super-strength **FIRST APPEARANCE:** *Infinite Frontier* Vol 1 #0 (May 2021) **SUBSIDIARY CATEGORY:** Magical

Levi Kamei is chosen as the new Swamp Thing on a trip back to his native India after being connected to the forests through a ritual his mother conducted. He and his brother are anointed to be the keepers of the old ways of their tribal lands, the protectors of the ancient forest. Levi is connected to the Green, a living network of information, and as a consequence can communicate with and control plant life. Unlike his predecessor Alec Holland, the new Swamp Thing is not an ambulatory plant being animated by the essence of a human, but a still-living human who can transform between forms with increasing levels of control.

BLACK ORCHID

19	St
Oh	
Black Orchid	

REAL NAME: Alba Garcia **POWERS:** Connection to the Red and the Green enables shape-shifting, chlorokinesis **FIRST APPEARANCE:** *Adventure Comics* Vol 1 #428 (Aug 1973) **SUBSIDIARY CATEGORY:** Lab Created

Black Orchid is an highly unusual individual as she has a connection to both the Red and the Green. A former army private who has lost both her arms, Alba Garcia agrees to take part in a top-secret program known as Project Ascension, which connects her to the elemental life forces on Earth so that she can acquire all the powers that go along with that, including control over animals and vegetation. Alba can also shape-shift, which allows her to fashion new limbs for herself. With her unique abilities, she takes on the name Black Orchid and becomes a very important asset for A.R.G.U.S. (Advanced Research Group Uniting Super-Humans), and is later assigned to the Justice League Dark.

ANCILLARY EXEMPLARS

47	Ba
Pt	
Parliament of Trees	

52	Ba
Lm	
Parliament of Limbs	

53	Tx
Pa	
Parliament of Decay	

Eons ago, the Lords of Order convened the forces of the natural world, and various Parliaments were formed to oversee them and choose their Avatars, known collectively as the Parliaments of Life. They include the **Parliament of Trees**, a council governing the living Green made up of all previous Avatars of that elemental force, a hive mind of every plant elemental that has ever existed. The **Parliament of Limbs** is the equivalent body for the Red, a collective of all spirits of animal Avatars. Opposing these life forces is the Rot, or the Black, represented by the **Parliament of Decay**, and its champions are Avatars of Death. The forces of Life must fight against the Rot, but Death must still be a part of Life for balance to be maintained.

SOLOMON GRUNDY

REAL NAME: Cyrus Gold **POWERS:** Super-strength, durability, stamina; resurrection **FIRST APPEARANCE:** *All-American Comics* Vol 1 #61 (Oct 1944) **SUBSIDIARY CATEGORY:** Metals

5	Vo
So	
Solomon Grundy	

When Cyrus Gold dies and his body sinks into Slaughter Swamp near Gotham City, his existence is far from over. The swamp is imbued with an elemental energy that causes Cyrus to rise again decades later as a zombie, an animated corpse partially composed of plant matter from around where its body lay. With little to no memory of its previous life, this being adopts the name Solomon Grundy after hearing the famous nursery rhyme. It is possible that Slaughter Swamp contains some Dionesium, the life-restoring metal originating from the Dark Multiverse that is found in Lazarus Pits, as there is a large subterranean reservoir of the substance found under nearby Gotham City, which may have leached into the surrounding soil. Solomon Grundy is at the same time dead and unkillable, as he will always rise again out of Slaughter Swamp after "dying."

KING SHARK

REAL NAME: Nanaue **POWERS:** Super-strength, durability, stamina, speed; enhanced senses; amphibious nature; limb regeneration **FIRST APPEARANCE:** *Superboy* Vol 4 #9 (Nov 1994) **SUBSIDIARY CATEGORY:** Divine, Lab Created

31	Vo
Ks	
King Shark	

King Shark is a super-strong hybrid of human and god, resembling in appearance and power set the marine animal for which he is named. He can swim exceptionally fast, withstand the pressures of the deep ocean, and aims to end every battle by literally devouring his opponent. Thanks to the human portion of his DNA, he can also survive on land. Like a shark, if he scents blood it can trigger a frenzy state in King Shark. His father is the powerful Hawaiian shark deity Kamo, and King Shark is taken as a child from his home to be raised in laboratory conditions as a weapon for the Suicide Squad. Kamo, a member of the Parliament of Limbs governing the Red, intends for King Shark to become the Exemplar of the Sea, its greatest warrior.

ANTON ARCANE

REAL NAME: Anton Arcane **POWERS:** Control over life cycle of living things; magic **FIRST APPEARANCE:** *Swamp Thing* Vol 1 #2 (Jan 1973) **SUBSIDIARY CATEGORY:** Magical

Anton Arcane is the Avatar of the Rot, appointed by the Parliament of Decay. Chosen due to his twisted personality, he is obsessed with death. His task is to help decay gain ascendancy over life on Earth, as represented by the Green and the Red. He is given the power to control the life cycle of any living thing, specifically causing putrefaction and death. Anton seeks immortality for himself by taking over other bodies. His appearance is too decayed for him to pass unnoticed by regular humans so he creates synthetic bodies for this purpose, turning any that do not make the grade into "Un-Men," his mindless servants. Even without his Rot powers, Anton is skilled in magic and science.

ABBY ARCANE

REAL NAME: Abigail Arcane **POWERS:** Control over life cycle of living things; metamorphosis **FIRST APPEARANCE:** *Swamp Thing* Vol 1 #3 (Mar 1973) **SUBSIDIARY CATEGORY:** Metagenetic Manifestation

The niece of Anton Arcane, Abby unwillingly inherits his title of Avatar of the Rot. She is touched by the Rot from birth, infecting her mother with it as a baby. Abby fights the influence of the forces of Decay, even killing another Avatar, but eventually she is forced to accept her role as the Black Queen of Death to stop her insane uncle from having too much power. As Avatar, Abby can reshape parts of her body as needed, including growing wings for flight and regenerating lost limbs. She also has control over the life cycle of living things, being able to cause rot or death within them. Despite representing opposite forces of nature, Abby Arcane and Swamp Thing (Alec Holland) develop feelings for each other, and have a daughter together.

ANCILLARY EXEMPLARS

Another example of a hybrid of human and marine animal is **Orca**, although she is not born this way. Instead, she develops powers and appearance resembling a killer whale after merging her DNA with that of an orca in order to cure a terrible injury. Like the Avatars of the Rot, **Black Hand** is a villain who can control the dead, raising an army of zombies in service to his master Nekron, the manifestation of Death. **Brother Blood**, on the other hand, is obsessed with the living and wishes to gain access to the powers of the Red. He tries to do this by practicing dark blood magic rituals, including bathing in blood to maintain his youth and strength.

FIRESTORM

REAL NAME: Ronnie Raymond, Dr. Martin Stein, and Jason Rusch **POWERS:** Power over molecules enables super-strength, durability, stamina, speed, flight, energy absorption and blasts, enhanced senses **FIRST APPEARANCE:** *Firestorm the Nuclear Man* Vol 1 #1 (Mar 1978) **SUBSIDIARY CATEGORY:** Lab Created

Firestorm is the result of the fusion of two consciousnesses into one hero within the Firestorm Matrix, a physical possibility created by Professor Martin Stein's research into the so-called "God Particle." As Firestorm, teenagers Ronnie Raymond and Jason Rusch, and sometimes Stein himself, combine their brawn and brain, with Ronnie as the "driver" of the body and the professor or Jason as the "passenger," a voice in Ronnie's head giving advice. Also known as the Nuclear Man, Firestorm can control the molecules of all substances, triggering a wide range of powers such as flight, transmutation, and creating energy blasts. However, the nature of their abilities also means that Firestorm can be unstable, and if too many individuals try to access the Matrix at one time, a catastrophic nuclear explosion can occur.

CAPTAIN ATOM

REAL NAME: Nathaniel Adam **POWERS:** Draws energy from Quantum Field to gain super-strength, durability, stamina, speed; fires quantum blasts **FIRST APPEARANCE:** *Captain Atom* Vol 2 #1 (Mar 1987) **SUBSIDIARY CATEGORY:** Lab Created

Captain Atom gets his incredible powers from the Quantum Field, the space containing the essence of all matter and energy. After an experiment he has volunteered for goes awry, he becomes a being of pure energy, a living nuclear dynamo, his atoms splitting and reforming constantly. This produces so much energy that sometimes he expels it involuntarily, presenting a serious risk to anyone within blast range. One day, Captain Atom expels so much energy that he is sent through the Quantum Field into the past; when he returns to his own time after five years, the process has stabilized his corporal structure and he can now switch between his quantum form and his human body. In the former, he can draw upon the limitless energy within the Quantum Field to gain super-strength, or fire blasts of quantum energy.

BUMBLEBEE

REAL NAME: Karen Beecher **POWERS:** Energy blasts; suit gives ability to fly and shrink **FIRST APPEARANCE:** *Teen Titans* Vol 1 #45 (Dec 1976) **SUBSIDIARY CATEGORY:** Amazing Armor and Wondrous Weapons

Karen Beecher's powers appear suddenly when she is pregnant with her first child, possibly as a result of exposure to radioactive Zeta Beams. Feeling an energy buzzing inside her, she finds that she has super-speed and can also channel the energy through her hands to fire blasts. Her armored suit enables her to further hone and control her powers, including being able to fly and shrink to a very small size. Her emerging powers attract the interest of the evil organization H.I.V.E., who have devised a way of stealing the powers of metahumans to resell to others. Although she fights alongside The Titans for a time, Karen eventually retires from the life of a Super Hero to spend more time with her family.

NEGATIVE MAN

REAL NAME: Larry Trainor **POWERS:** In negative spirit form is intangible, can absorb and fire out energy, and fly **FIRST APPEARANCE:** *My Greatest Adventure* Vol 1 #80 (Jun 1963)

Without his knowledge, Larry Trainor is deliberately exposed to radiation by Dr. Niles Caulder, who is trying to build his Doom Patrol Super Hero team. Larry becomes Negative Man after merging with a being comprised of negative energy. This connection enables him to send his consciousness out as an intangible negative spirit—but Larry risks death if it is for more than 60 seconds. As Negative Man, he can fly, give off explosive blasts, and pass through solid objects. Larry's human form is left highly radioactive by his accident, so Caulder designs bandages that he can wear to protect those close to him. Larry later loses his connection with his negative spirit and becomes Positive Man.

ANCILLARY EXEMPLARS

The villain **Multiplex** gains his powers in the same explosion that creates the hero Firestorm. Multiplex experiences fission, the ability to split himself into duplicates, which he calls his duploids. Another villain triggered by radioactivity is **Parasite** (Rudy Jones). While working as a janitor at S.T.A.R. Labs, Rudy acquires the ability to siphon off the powers of others, which he can convert into energy to strengthen himself. Radiation also changes **Doctor Phosphorus**. Formerly a nuclear scientist, he is covered in radioactive sand, causing him to move him one element along from sand on the periodic table, from silicon to phosphorus. His skin becomes transparent and he constantly emits radiation.

RAY

REAL NAME: Raymond Terrill **POWERS:** Absorption of light energy to fly, fire blasts, make himself and others invisible, create light constructs **FIRST APPEARANCE:** *The Ray* Vol 1 #1 (Feb 1992) **SUBSIDIARY CATEGORY:** Metagenetic Manifestation

Ray Terrill is born with a metagene inherited from his father that allows his body to absorb and utilize energy from any kind of light—natural light, direct sunlight, and even artificial lighting. At first he believes that he is allergic to light and he is kept locked up for his own safety, but after he escapes the house as an angry teenager, he realizes that this is not the case. He is not allergic to light, but rather he absorbs it, and if the energy is not expelled somehow, he can suddenly explode and hurt someone. Ray learns that he can expel his light powers and keep them at safe levels by bending light around himself, which makes him invisible; he can also make other people and objects invisible. As well as this ability, he can create light constructs and fly.

RAY

REAL NAME: Langford "Happy" Terrill **POWERS:** Absorption of light energy to fly and fire blasts; ability to make himself and others invisible, create light constructs, and transform into a pure energy being **FIRST APPEARANCE:** *Smash Comics* Vol 1 #14 (Sep 1940) **SUBSIDIARY CATEGORY:** Accidental

Langford "Happy" Terrill is Ray Terrill's father, and the first Super Hero to be known as the Ray. He is unwittingly exposed to a "light bomb," giving him the power to absorb light energy and convert it into various superpowers, including flight, firing energy blasts, invisibility, and creating hard-light constructs. Happy can also communicate in secret with others by vibrating their inner ears with his solid light constructs. By converting his body into pure light energy, Happy can become invulnerable, travel through deep space without being harmed, and move at the speed of light. As the Ray, he often works under the auspices of the government, who are playing a long game by predicting that his children will inherit his abilities genetically and therefore be useful to them.

DOCTOR LIGHT

REAL NAME: Arthur Light **POWERS:** As a being of pure energy, he is invulnerable to attack and can create hard-light constructs **FIRST APPEARANCE:** *Justice League of America* Vol 1 #12 (Jun 1962) **SUBSIDIARY CATEGORY:** Accidental, Genius Intelligence

Arthur Light is an A.R.G.U.S. scientist, an expert on metahuman physics, who is exposed to radiation, which gives him the ability to drain energy from external sources. This allows him suck the light out of every room he is in. After a spell with the Justice League of America—trying to be a hero— Light dies after Superman's heat vision is accidentally triggered, but returns as a being of pure light energy. Formerly a good man, in his light ghost form, Doctor Light seeks revenge for what happened to him, feeling that everything went wrong when he chose to be a hero. He guards his remote island lair with hard-light constructs, which he creates by circulating light photon particles in the same way as atoms move in a solid. Arthur's wife, Kimiyo Hoshi, also takes on the moniker of Doctor Light, although she is consistently a hero and derives her powers from the Source, an energy linked to The Presence.

SOLARIS

REAL NAME: Solaris **POWERS:** Energy absorption and radiation; gravitational pull; supercomputer hardware and functioning **FIRST APPEARANCE:** *DC One Million* Vol 1 #1 (Nov 1998) **SUBSIDIARY CATEGORY:** Constructed Beings

Solaris is an artificial sun existing in the 853rd century, built to bring heat and light to the outer limits of Earth's solar system. However, this massive supercomputer becomes insane as a result of a techno-virus inputted into it by itself via a time loop. The newly sentient Solaris decides to destroy Superman, and absorbs 300 other suns into its core to build up enough power to do this. Although very few entities have the capability of taking on Solaris the Tyrant Sun, occasionally it is defeated. When this happens, Solaris enters a shutdown mode and processes what it has learned from the encounter in order to trigger an upgrade that will enable it to overcome the same attack next time.

STARMAN

REAL NAME: William Payton **POWERS:** Energy from Totality gives flight, ability to fire blasts, and open portals **FIRST APPEARANCE:** *Starman* Vol 1 #1 (Oct 1988) **SUBSIDIARY CATEGORY:** Accidental

Will Payton acquires unimaginable cosmic power by complete happenstance. He is out hiking when a blast of energy from a malfunctioning satellite strikes him. This satellite has been absorbing radiation from an approaching energy source known as the Totality, thought to be the cause of the Big Bang that created the Multiverse itself. Overloaded, the satellite's systems cannot cope, and Will is imbued with a tiny piece of the Totality. Its energy courses through him, immediately obvious in his white, glowing eyes. He now has access to limitless energy, enabling him to fly, open portals to anywhere in the Multiverse, and fire powerful cosmic blasts. He also wields the Cosmic Staff to channel these powers.

Although he uses his new abilities to become a hero, Starman is inevitably a target of those who want to know more about the Totality, whether for good or bad purposes. Lex Luthor kidnaps him from his time and brings him to the 21st century, where Luthor stops at nothing to extract information from him. By studying the Totality, answers can be found to how and when the Multiverse was built, and by whom.

COSMIC CONNECTION

Will has cosmic awareness, the Totality connecting him to every corner of the Multiverse. He also has a more specific link to every being who has held the title of Starman, past, present, and future. In the battle against the dark forces of Perpetua, Will uses this connection to unite the fragments of the Totality by opening star-shaped portals to let all the Starmen merge their powers. However, even this is not enough to defeat Perpetua, and she kills Will in retaliation.

Starman's connection to the energy of the cosmos also links him to all the Starmen who have ever existed or will ever exist, like a constellation across time and space.

CYBORG SUPERMAN

30   Vo
Cs
Cyborg
Superman

REAL NAME: Hank Henshaw **POWERS:** Super-strength, durability, stamina, speed, agility, reflexes; flight; heat vision; freeze breath **FIRST APPEARANCE:** *The Adventures of Superman* Vol 1 #500 (Jun 1993) **SUBSIDIARY CATEGORY:** Constructed Beings, Alien Origins, Genius Intelligence

Hank Henshaw is on a space mission when cosmic radiation engulfs his craft. He and his crew are mutated into monstrous beings, who Superman later fights. Eventually Hank's body dies, but his consciousness lives on, and he uses it to inhabit technology in order to begin a new kind of existence. Blaming Superman for his plight, Hank employs his scientific genius to construct a new body for himself that will be capable of matching and even defeating the Man of Steel. The result is Cyborg Superman, a blend of cloned Kryptonian organic matter and advanced technology. Like all Kryptonians, Cyborg Superman's powers are enhanced under a yellow sun.

HEAT WAVE

11   Co
He
Heat Wave

REAL NAME: Mick Rory **POWERS:** Pyrokinesis; heat gun fires concentrated blasts **FIRST APPEARANCE:** *The Flash* Vol 1 #140 (Nov 1963) **SUBSIDIARY CATEGORY:** Amazing Armor and Wondrous Weapons

Pyromaniac Mick Rory builds a life of crime based around his affinity with fire, usually wielding a heat gun. His power set receives an incredible boost when he gains a connection to the Sage Force. This cosmic energy makes him a powerful telepath, able to project illusions into the minds of others. When his Sage Force comes into contact with the Speed Force of The Flash (Barry Allen), Mick becomes dangerously unstable, with the risk of a deadly flare of Sage energy. Only a future version of his old friend Captain Cold can calm Mick down enough for him to mentally reject the Sage Force, and once it is purged from his body, Heat Wave finds the burn scars he has carried since childhood all healed.

IMPERIEX

34   Vo
Ix
Imperiex

REAL NAME: Imperiex **POWERS:** Wields cosmic energy, super-strength and durability; creates black holes **FIRST APPEARANCE:** *Superman* Vol 2 #153 (Feb 2000) **SUBSIDIARY CATEGORY:** Alien Origins, Sphere of the Gods

Imperiex is a being representing the living force of entropy, the natural law of physics that dictates that systems will always decline into chaos. He is comprised of pure energy, which needs to be contained within some kind of outer shell in order for him to assume a coherent form. This is why Imperiex is usually seen wearing a vast suit of armor. If this is destroyed, Imperiex still exists, but dissipates as energy until another shell can be made. He wields enormous power and is said to be able to create and destroy universes by triggering Big Bangs. He can also manifest black holes and fashion android probes resembling smaller versions of himself. He is known as Imperiex-Prime to differentiate himself from these duplicates.

BLACK LIGHTNING

REAL NAME: Jefferson Pierce **POWERS:** Electrokinesis enables firing electric blasts, creation of electromagnetic force fields, flight **FIRST APPEARANCE:** *Black Lightning* Vol 1 #1 (Apr 1977) **SUBSIDIARY CATEGORY:** Metagenetic Manifestation

20   Ba

Bl

Black Lightning

Jefferson Pierce is a teacher who is also a metahuman, with the power to generate and channel electricity. He is trained in the use of his powers and in general combat techniques from an early age by his father, a journalist, and Amberjack, a reformed villain turned hero. He also spends time with the Justice League, where he picks up more tips for taking on villains.

Jefferson can use electromagnetic forces to push himself into the air and "fly," a technique Cyborg teaches him. He can also create force fields that protect him from bullets even at close range, the electromagnetism in his body responding to threats even before he has consciously realized they are there. Additionally, his electrical powers can be used to disable nearby communications devices. His suit can absorb blows to reduce their impact, and is made for him by the mysterious "illegal alien" and actual shape-shifting extraterrestrial, Usagi. The suit can also be made bright or dark depending on what the situation requires, and it can render Jefferson's face blurry to anyone trying

to film or take pictures of him, to protect his secret identity. This effect even works to some degree on normal human vision. Jefferson also has the ability to fire electric blasts or produce balls of electricity to hurl at opponents.

ELECTRIC CITY

Jefferson returns to his hometown to try and make his old neighborhood Brick City a better place, both as a teacher and a hero. Although he finds himself clashing with police almost as much as with criminals, Black Lightning is determined that he will do everything he can to give the people of Brick City safe streets and brighter futures.

By mastering the potential of electromagnetic force, Black Lightning can channel it into both offensive and defensive uses.

LIGHTNING

35	St
Lg	
Lightning	

REAL NAME: Jennifer Pierce **POWERS:** Electrokinesis enables firing electric blasts, creation of electromagnetic force fields, flight **FIRST APPEARANCE:** *Justice Society of America* Vol 3 #12 (Mar 2008) **SUBSIDIARY CATEGORY:** Metagenetic Manifestation

A blood relative of Black Lightning (Jefferson Pierce), Jennifer Pierce also has a metagene granting her electric powers. This means that she, like Jefferson, can create electrical energy from her own body and manipulate it into blasts and force fields. Since Jennifer is still young, she has not been trained extensively like Jefferson, and her lack of experience means that she is not ready to hit the streets to take on bad guys. Her sister Anissa also has powers that she has not yet learned to master, and Jefferson is keen that both girls hold off on any kind of heroic activity until they have graduated from school.

JENNY SPARKS

32	St
Jn	
Jenny Sparks	

REAL NAME: Jenny Sparks **POWERS:** Total control of electricity to fire blasts and become an energy being; decelerated aging **FIRST APPEARANCE:** *StormWatch* Vol 1 #37 (Jul 1996) **SUBSIDIARY CATEGORY:** Metagenetic Manifestation

Jenny Sparks has the power to control electricity and she is also a Century Baby— one of several people born on January 1, 1900, and fated to die on December 31, 1999. All Century Babies develop superhuman powers during their lives. Jenny stops aging when she is 19 years old and retains her appearance decades later. With her extensive electrical powers, Jenny can turn into a being of pure electrical energy. In this state she can travel anywhere that electricity can, via power lines and electrical devices. She does not generate electricity herself, however, and all her powers must be channeled through external sources.

ANCILLARY EXEMPLARS

51	Co
Lw	
Livewire	

46	Co
Db	
Deathbolt	

44	Co
El	
Electrocutioner	

49	St
Vh	
Static	

Livewire is a vlogger who is turned into a being of pure energy when a prank goes wrong. **Deathbolt** is an unwilling electricity-wielder—his plane is struck by lightning and he is experimented on by the deranged scientist Ultra-Humanite until he becomes a living battery. A villain by choice, the **Electrocutioner** has no powers, but wears a powerful electrokinetic suit. Virgil Hawkins becomes the electricity-generating hero **Static** after a chemical explosion. The chemical, Quantum Juice, proves fatal to most, but a few so-called "Bang Babies" gain powers from the incident.

EARTH ELEMENTS: TABULATION

OTHER-DIMENSIONAL

The Multiverse contains many different universes where alternate realities play out. However, there are also places beyond even these, where sometimes strange and twisted beings gather and wait for a chance to cross over.

Ae ALTERNATIVE EARTHS

In each universe there is a version of planet Earth, where events take unexpected turns and both heroes and villains have divergent stories.

4	Vo
Cr	
Crime Syndicate	

10	St
By	
Batman Beyond	

8	St
Wv	
Waverider	

5	St
K	
Kamandi	

12	St
Ji	
Justice Incarnate	

6	St
Pg	
Power Girl	

19	St
Na	
Naomi	

11	St
Vz	
Superman (Val-Zod)	

Fd FIFTH DIMENSION

The Fifth Dimension is a place existing beyond the space-time continuum and populated by bizarre reality-bending entities.

2	Vo
Mz	
Mr. Mxyzptlk	

3	Vo
Vb	
Bat-Mite	

1	Vo
Yz	
Yz the Thunderbolt	

SIXTH DIMENSION

The Sixth Dimension is the highest plane of existence in the Multiverse, acting as a control room for the other dimensions.

DARK MULTIVERSE

The Dark Multiverse is a twisted reflection of the primary Multiverse, populated by worlds that are deemed unfit for existence.

CRIME SYNDICATE

REAL NAME: Various **POWERS:** Various **FIRST APPEARANCE:** *Justice League of America* Vol 1 #29 (Aug 1964)

4 Vo

Cr

Crime Syndicate

The Multiverse contains many different versions of the planet Earth, and for every different Earth, there are different iterations of the heroic Justice League and their allies who protect Prime Earth. The existence of the Multiverse means that there are potential "lifeboat" realities available to those whose own worlds are destroyed, as long as they have the means to cross over the boundaries between universes. This is something that the Crime Syndicate of Earth-Three take advantage of. They are not courageous protectors of the innocent like the Justice League, but self-serving, vain, ambitious, and just plain evil. Their twisted worldview is not unusual on Earth-Three, a corrupt and morally bankrupt planet where brute strength rules. Here, the natural order of things is for the Crime Syndicate to use their powers to crush weaker beings underfoot, but while they are in theory an alliance, it is a union built on mistrust and personal ambition.

Unlike the Justice League, the Crime Syndicate can use their powers with total freedom, as they do not care about collateral damage, whether of infrastructure or people.

DARK MIRROR

While their motivations and personalities are very different, almost opposites to their Justice League counterparts, the powers of the Crime Syndicate align almost exactly. Ultraman is the equivalent to Superman, and shares his incredible super-strength, durability, speed, and stamina, as well as the powers of flight, heat vision, and freeze breath. However, unlike the Man of Steel, Ultraman's powers are strengthened by Kryptonite and weakened by a yellow sun. He values strength above anything, and despises anyone he sees as weak.

Owlman is Thomas Wayne Jr., who inherits the family fortune after the killings of his parents and younger brother, Bruce.

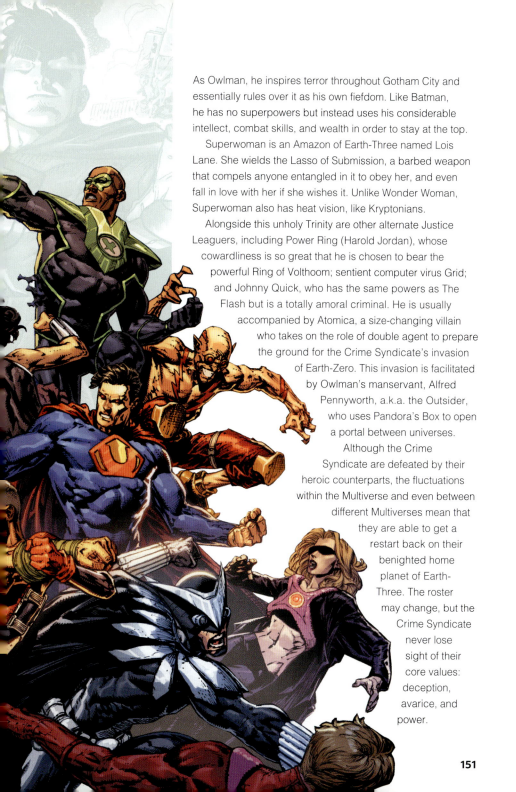

As Owlman, he inspires terror throughout Gotham City and essentially rules over it as his own fiefdom. Like Batman, he has no superpowers but instead uses his considerable intellect, combat skills, and wealth in order to stay at the top.

Superwoman is an Amazon of Earth-Three named Lois Lane. She wields the Lasso of Submission, a barbed weapon that compels anyone entangled in it to obey her, and even fall in love with her if she wishes it. Unlike Wonder Woman, Superwoman also has heat vision, like Kryptonians.

Alongside this unholy Trinity are other alternate Justice Leaguers, including Power Ring (Harold Jordan), whose cowardliness is so great that he is chosen to bear the powerful Ring of Volthoom; sentient computer virus Grid; and Johnny Quick, who has the same powers as The Flash but is a totally amoral criminal. He is usually accompanied by Atomica, a size-changing villain who takes on the role of double agent to prepare the ground for the Crime Syndicate's invasion of Earth-Zero. This invasion is facilitated by Owlman's manservant, Alfred Pennyworth, a.k.a. the Outsider, who uses Pandora's Box to open a portal between universes.

Although the Crime Syndicate are defeated by their heroic counterparts, the fluctuations within the Multiverse and even between different Multiverses mean that they are able to get a restart back on their benighted home planet of Earth-Three. The roster may change, but the Crime Syndicate never lose sight of their core values: deception, avarice, and power.

BATMAN BEYOND

REAL NAME: Terry McGinnis **ABILITIES:** Prodigious intellect; expert in martial arts and technology **FIRST APPEARANCE:** *Batman Beyond* Vol 1 #1 (Nov 1999) **SUBSIDIARY CATEGORY:** Genius Intelligence, Amazing Armor and Wondrous Weapons

Teenager Terry McGinnis has taken on the role of Batman in a possible future version of Gotham City, Neo-Gotham, where Bruce Wayne is retired and has—eventually—given Terry his blessing. Like his mentor, Terry has no metahuman powers, but he possesses a high intellect, and is skilled in hand-to-hand combat thanks to intensive training from Bruce himself. Perhaps worth just as much is the advice that Terry gets from Bruce on how to be the Batman that Neo-Gotham needs— to always have the right tool for the job, to train all the time to try and be better, and to honehis skills so that they become instinctive.

FUTURE TECH

As befits a Batman of the future, Terry's Batsuit is packed with cutting-edge tech. Unlike that of the original Batman, this includes flight capability via rocket-fuel-powered thrusters in the boots and aided by gliding wings fitted along the arms. It also deploys a vast array of AI capabilities to ensure that Terry is ready for any situation—passive proximity sensors to constantly monitor his surroundings and prepare accordingly, a transmitter array that can tune in to any communication device in the city, and a memory core that backs up all gathered metadata for analysis. The suit also has a targeted camouflage response to the surrounding area. It is later upgraded to include hard-light features, including Batarangs. Terry understands that Batman's legacy is to be a symbol in the dark, inspiring ordinary citizens to have hope and never give up fighting for what is right.

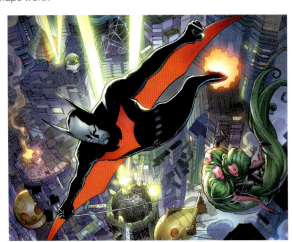

Terry's futuristic Batsuit, later upgraded to feature hard-light wings, enables him to soar above the dark streets of Neo-Gotham.

WAVERIDER

REAL NAME: Matthew Ryder **POWERS:** Time travel; precognition; flight; invisibility; intangibility; fires quantum energy blasts **FIRST APPEARANCE:** *Armageddon* 2001 Vol 1 #1 (May 1991) **SUBSIDIARY CATEGORY:** Energies: Cosmic

Matthew Ryder is a scientist from an alternate future in which a tyrannical being named Monarch has destroyed all Super Heroes. Matthew volunteers for an experiment that will enable him to travel back in time and prevent his present from happening. As a result, he acquires superpowers by being merged with the timestream, otherwise known as the Fourth Dimension. He is able to travel through time via the Quantum Field, either forward or backward. Additionally, Matthew can temporarily possess other people to glimpse their probable futures. Believing Monarch to be a former hero, Matthew uses his abilities to deduce which hero will one day turn into the despot, and prevent that occurring. Matthew can also fire quantum blasts, become invisible and intangible, and fly at light speed.

KAMANDI

REAL NAME: Unknown **ABILITIES:** Survival skills, including tracking and basic combat **FIRST APPEARANCE:** *Kamandi* Vol 1 #1 (Nov 1972)

Kamandi is the "last boy on Earth," living on a planet devastated by a Great Disaster. This catastrophe has almost wiped out the human race. It also releases radiation that merges with experimental drugs being used on animal species, causing them to evolve and mutate into bipedal, talking beings, frequently at war with each other. The surviving humans have conversely devolved and become a slave society for their animal masters. Kamandi himself is raised by androids in a protective bunker designated Command D—his name is merely a misinterpretation of this, his real name being unknown. Although he has no metahuman powers, Kamandi has learned to survive on his skills alone in a demanding environment. As the last human alive with his natural intelligence intact, he fights a lone battle until he encounters the reality-hopping Justice League.

JUSTICE INCARNATE

REAL NAME: Various **POWERS:** Various **FIRST APPEARANCE:** *The Multiversity* Vol 1 #2 (Jun 2015)

Justice Incarnate is a unique team of heroes comprising the most powerful warriors for good from across the Multiverse. Showcasing a wide range of abilities, these heroes are brought together via a signal sent out from the former home of the Monitors, an immensely powerful group of beings who watch over every universe and timestream in existence. This signal is designed only to be sent when the Monitors have all disappeared and there is an existential threat to the Multiverse. The Monitors' base is located in the Fifth Dimension, where it rotates around a fixed point in the Bleed, the life force of the Multiverse. It serves as a watchtower in the Orrery of Worlds, an alternate term for the Multiverse. Each version of Earth in the Multiverse occupies the same space, but is vibrating at a different frequency—the Monitors have the technology to tune in to those frequencies using their ship, the *Ultima Thule*, and using this method they can travel anywhere in the Multiverse.

HOUSE OF HEROES

When Justice Incarnate take over this base, they rename it the House of Heroes, and use it to surveil all realities and watch for threats.

The group's natural leader is the Superman of Earth-23, Calvin Ellis, who, in his own reality, also juggles the job of being US President with that of being a Super Hero. He is joined by the Aquawoman of Earth-11; the storm god Thunderer of Earth-Seven; Dino-Cop of Earth-41, Earth-Five's Mary Marvel, and Captain Carrot; a rabbit hero from Earth-26 whose world is governed by cartoon physics. Along with other Multiversal heroes from 50 worlds, this powerful team makes up a volunteer army ready to fight cosmic-level threats wherever they should appear.

The members of Justice Incarnate have varying knowledge of each other's worlds, with some even claiming that their adventures are recorded for posterity in comic books.

POWER GIRL

REAL NAME: Kara Zor-L **POWERS:** Super-strength, speed, durability, stamina, senses; flight; heat vision; freeze breath **FIRST APPEARANCE:** *All Star Comics* Vol 1 #58 (Feb 1976) **SUBSIDIARY CATEGORY:** Alien Origins, Energies: Light

Kara Zor-L is originally from the Krypton of her reality, but becomes a hero on the world designated Earth-Two, taking the name Power Girl. Cousin to Kal-L, the Superman of that reality, Kara joins the Justice Society when he retires. In terms of her biology and therefore her power set, as Kryptonians get their powers directly from their natural physiology under a yellow sun, Kara is identical to her Earth-Zero counterpart, Supergirl. She is super-strong, durable, and speedy, and has heat vision and freeze breath. Unlike Supergirl, Power Girl has also successfully run her own company. Kara has survived multiple crises and changes to reality and is now based on Earth-Zero with her Justice Society teammates from Earth-Two.

NAOMI

REAL NAME: Naomi McDuffie **POWERS:** Super-strength, durability, stamina, speed, senses; energy powers; flight **FIRST APPEARANCE:** *Naomi* Vol 1 #1 (Mar 2019) **SUBSIDIARY CATEGORY:** Metagenetic Manifestation

Naomi McDuffie lives on Earth-Zero, but she is not from that reality. In fact, it is not known which part of the Multiverse the powerful teenager is from, only that she was sent away from it for her own protection. She is raised by adoptive parents, one of whom is from the planet Rann, but she inherits her godlike superpowers from her parents, who in turn got them when their Earth was bathed in mysterious radioactive energies. Her powers include the ability to project intense energy blasts and fly, as well as incredible levels of super-strength and durability. When Naomi fires up her powers, golden armor manifests on her body.

SUPERMAN

REAL NAME: Val-Zod **POWERS:** Super-strength, speed, durability, stamina, reflexes, senses; flight; heat vision; freeze breath **FIRST APPEARANCE:** *Earth 2* Vol 1 #19 (Mar 2014) **SUBSIDIARY CATEGORY:** Alien Origins, Energies: Light, Genius Intelligence

Val-Zod is a native Kryptonian who escapes his dying planet and ends up on Earth-Two. As he possesses all the natural abilities of a Kryptonian under a yellow sun, he finds himself to be extraordinarily powerful on his new homeworld. At first Val-Zod is reluctant to use his powers in the outside world, as his long voyage through space in a capsule has left him agoraphobic; however, he also spent that time studying the vast reserves of Kryptonian knowledge to which he has access, which has left him with an advanced intellect. When the original Superman of Earth-Two falls, Val faces his fears and steps up to take his mantle as the protector of his Earth.

MR. MXYZPTLK

REAL NAME: Unpronounceable **POWERS:** Near omnipotence; reality-altering powers; immortality; vast knowledge; teleportation **FIRST APPEARANCE:** *Superman* Vol 1 #30 (Oct 1944) **SUBSIDIARY CATEGORY:** Metagenetic Manifestation

Mr. Mxyzptlk is one of the Multiverse's more unusual beings. He is a phenomenally powerful entity known as an imp, from the Fifth Dimension. Mxyzptlk himself describes the Fifth Dimension as being a place that is pure imagination, somewhere that is around us all the time but is not usually perceptible to ordinary beings. The Fifth Dimension exists beyond the first four dimensions, beyond even time itself.

MAKING MISCHIEF

Mr. Mxyzptlk is unusual not only because of the nature of his powers, but how he chooses to use them. When he visits Earth-Zero, often to torment Superman, he has near limitless abilities to alter reality itself. While his antics appear to most people as magic, Mxyzptlk instead sees them as the science of the Fifth Dimension in action, since it is a place where the usual laws of physics do not apply. He can transport himself anywhere in the Multiverse, and has near unrivaled knowledge of the cosmos. He is functionally immortal as he can use his powers to recover from most injuries instantly. But Mr. Mxyzptlk

is not interested in pushing his powers to their full potential in order to destroy, or to gain power for himself—he likes to use them to joke around and have fun. However, even the imp's idea of fun can be dangerous, and Superman often has to employ Mr. Mxyzptlk's one vulnerability— he is banished back to the Fifth Dimension if he can be tricked or persuaded into saying his own name backward.

Mr. Mxyzptlk claims that he is really a kind of guardian angel to Superman, although he enjoys teasing him.

BAT-MITE

REAL NAME: Unknown **POWERS:** Near omnipotence; reality-altering powers; immortality; vast knowledge; teleportation **FIRST APPEARANCE:** *Detective Comics* Vol 1 #267 (May 1959) **SUBSIDIARY CATEGORY:** Metagenetic Manifestation

Bat-Mite is a mischievous "imp" from the Fifth Dimension who is fixated on Batman. In homage to his idol, he wears his own costume modeled on that of the Caped Crusader. Bat-Mite is supremely confident in his own abilities to be a Super Hero, and on being banished from his own dimension to Earth-Zero, starts calling Batman his sidekick. In fact, like any being from the Fifth Dimension, a realm of imagination where anything is possible, Bat-Mite possesses mind-bending powers. He can distort reality with his mind, teleport, and call on a vast range of abilities stemming from the advanced science of his dimension, which appears as unexplainable as magic to outsiders. However, he does not wish to use his powers for anything other than being a Super Hero like Batman and playing pranks.

YZ THE THUNDERBOLT

REAL NAME: Yz **POWERS:** Reality-altering; invisibility; intangibility; flight **FIRST APPEARANCE:** *The Flash* Vol 1 #1 (Jan 1940) **SUBSIDIARY CATEGORY:** Magical

Yz is a powerful genie from the Fifth Dimension, but he can apparently only access the full array of his abilities when bonded with and commanded by another being. Yz is formerly joined with the Justice Society's Johnny Thunder, who uses the summoning call "Cei-u!" to merge with the genie and become the heroic being Thunderbolt. Later, Yz inhabits a pen, found by Keystone City teen Jakeem Thunder, who summons the genie by saying, "So cool." Yz follows commands given to him by Johnny or Jakeem exactly, so they must be careful what they wish for— literally! Although Yz seems to be limited to following the rules of his confinement within objects and his loyalty to his bond with another, it is possible that this is an illusion and that he could be free if he so chooses.

PERPETUA

REAL NAME: Perpetua **POWERS:** Near omnipotent, with power to create Multiverses **FIRST APPEARANCE:** *Justice League* Vol 4 #8 (Nov 2018) **SUBSIDIARY CATEGORY:** Higher Powers

Perpetua is the progenitor of the Multiverse that existed before the current one, an unimaginably powerful being wielding the seven forces of creation. She is just one of a group called the Hands, Multiverse creators who came from the Omniverse, the space where all Multiverses that have ever existed or will ever exist originate. Beings such as her occupy a space known as the Sixth Dimension, a type of control room for the Multiverse that exists above all other dimensions. However, unlike the other Hands, Perpetua is not content to let herself be absorbed as energy back into the Source after creating her Multiverse. She goes rogue, and as a punishment for using her creation for selfish ends, she is imprisoned behind the Source Wall, her dark secrets hidden for billions of years.

ANTI-MONITOR

REAL NAME: Mobius **POWERS:** Immense superpowers fueled by absorbing the energy from destroyed universes; resurrection **FIRST APPEARANCE:** *Crisis on Infinite Earths* Vol 1 #2 (May 1985) **SUBSIDIARY CATEGORY:** Higher Powers

Mobius is a child of Perpetua, spawned to oversee the anti-matter universe, to guard the boundaries of creation and to keep them free of life. After she is shut away in the Source Wall, Mobius pledges to amass all the knowledge he needs to gain revenge on his brother Mar Novu, who he blames for taking away his domain and therefore his purpose. In pursuit of this goal, he builds the Mobius Chair to travel between dimensions and timestreams. Mobius later discovers the Anti-Life Equation, which has the power of life and death over sentient beings, and becomes its living embodiment, a powerful entity of destruction. Although Mobius's physiology and powers make him very difficult to harm, he can be killed; however, he is forever resurrected in the Sixth Dimension.

OVER-MONITOR

REAL NAME: Mar Novu **POWERS:** Immense superpowers, including advanced cosmic awareness; resurrection **FIRST APPEARANCE:** *The Batman Who Laughs* Vol 1 #1 (Jan 2018) **SUBSIDIARY CATEGORY:** Higher Powers

The Over-Monitor is created by his mother Perpetua to oversee the development of new worlds and universes, and prevent crises from occurring in them. As a Monitor, Mar Novu possesses powers almost beyond godlike, with exceptional levels of cosmic awareness and the ability to harness the energy of the positive-matter universe. He takes his role as watchman so seriously that, when he perceives that his mother poses a threat to the natural order of things, he marshals his brothers to act with him to stop her. This brings him into conflict with his brother Mobius, who is his natural opposite. Like his brothers, Mar Novu can be killed—with difficulty—but is then reborn within the Sixth Dimension.

WORLD FORGER

REAL NAME: Alpheus **POWERS:** Immense superpowers, including the ability to forge new universes with his hammer; resurrection **FIRST APPEARANCE:** *Dark Nights: Metal* Vol 1 #4 (Feb 2018) **SUBSIDIARY CATEGORY:** Higher Powers

Alpheus is created by Perpetua to occupy the Dark Multiverse and work a forge to make new worlds. If the worlds he forges are stable, they become part of the Multiverse, but if they are not, they are consumed by his creature Barbatos and their energies released back to him. As the World Forger, Alpheus wields a giant hammer, with which he generates the spark of creation to build new worlds, and as a Monitor, his range of superhuman powers includes energy absorption, shape- and size-changing, and the ability to spawn new universes. Alpheus tries to help the Justice League and their allies to defeat his mother when she becomes free of the Source Wall.

OBSERVER.IO

REAL NAME: Unknown **POWERS:** Reality-altering; flight; shape-changing; godlike physiology **FIRST APPEARANCE:** *Batman/Superman* Vol 2 #17 (Jun 2021) **SUBSIDIARY CATEGORY:** Divine

Observer.io is formerly the God of Tales, now forgotten by the peoples who used to worship him. He is the son of the World Forger, Alpheus. He wanders Earth for thousands of years until he comes upon a movie theater, which reminds him of the temples to which worshippers once flocked in his honor. When the rise of the internet makes cinemas less popular, the desire to create stories of his own forms into a tangible armor, encasing him. It destabilizes his mind as he seeks to use pieces of other worlds to create one perfect world of his own—the ultimate story. To do this, he assembles an archive of worlds and takes what he wants from them before disposing of them as "imperfect." After Superman and Batman reprogram his armor, he resolves to be merely an observer of worlds.

BATMAN WHO LAUGHS

REAL NAME: Bruce Wayne **POWERS:** Nigh omnipotence and omniscience after gaining extraordinary powers from a near-divine being **FIRST APPEARANCE:** *Dark Days: The Casting* #1 (Sep 2017) **SUBSIDIARY CATEGORY:** Accidental

14   Vo

WI

Batman Who Laughs

The Batman Who Laughs is an evil amalgam of Batman and The Joker, originating from Earth-22 in the Dark Multiverse. (Reality designations in the Dark Multiverse always carry a negative symbol before the number.)

Having accidentally inhaled Joker Venom in a struggle that also leads to The Joker's death in that reality, Batman loses his natural moral compass and becomes the scourge of Gotham City, and the rest of his world. Prior to that, he had the same abilities as Earth-Zero's Bruce Wayne—the brilliant mind, the rigorous training in various fighting styles, and other useful skills. The Batman Who Laughs personifies just how deadly Batman would be if he had no code of ethics. He later becomes one of the most formidable beings in any Multiverse when he acquires near transcendant powers from a godlike entity.

BARBATOS

REAL NAME: Barbatos **POWERS:** Extensive destructive powers; energy absorption; immortality; cosmic awareness **FIRST APPEARANCE:** *Dark Days: The Casting* #1 (Sep 2017) **SUBSIDIARY CATEGORY:** Metagenetic Manifestation

13   Re

Bs

Barbatos

Created to be like a pet for the World Forger, who creates worlds and beings for the Multiverse at his forge, Barbatos is a dragonlike creature that consumes the life energies of unstable planets to prevent

them from ascending to the Multiverse. The instinct to destroy becomes so powerful that Barbatos ends up killing the World Forger and deserting his purpose. This allows unstable worlds to live on, and these start proliferating in the Dark Multiverse. Barbatos then begins to hunger for the worlds of the Multiverse above, and plans an invasion of Earth-Zero to accomplish this, using Batman as a portal. Although he is exceedingly powerful and near invulnerable, it is possible to harm or restrain Barbatos with Tenth Metal, the purest form of creation from the World Forge.

DARK MONITOR

9	Vo
Di	
Dark Monitor	

REAL NAME: Dax Novu **POWERS:** As oldest Monitor, is a phenomenally powerful cosmic being; feeds on life energies **FIRST APPEARANCE:** *Final Crisis: Superman Beyond* Vol 1 #1 (Oct 2008) **SUBSIDIARY CATEGORY:** Higher Powers

Dax Novu is better known as Mandrakk, the Dark Monitor, a cosmic vampire who feeds on the Bleed, the substance found between universes. He is a corrupted Monitor who falls into the Dark Multiverse after being defeated by his son Nix Uotan and an army of Supermen from different realities. He attempts to break out to feed on the Bleed again, but after an encounter with the super-team the Unexpected, Mandrakk's physiology is altered. Now, instead of feeling hunger for positive life energies, he is given the biological imperative to consume dark energies, so for his own survival he is forced to remain in the Dark Multiverse and abandon his quest to leave it.

THE UPSIDE-DOWN MAN

17	Re
Ud	
The Upside-Down Man	

REAL NAME: None **POWERS:** Various dark magical powers, including eldritch blasts, interdimensional travel, shape-shifting, regeneration **FIRST APPEARANCE:** *Justice League Dark* Vol 2 #1 (Sep 2018) **SUBSIDIARY CATEGORY:** Magical

When magic is created, the light of its energy is formed into the being called Hecate; the Upside-Down Man is her opposite, formed from the darkness and inhabiting the Dark Multiverse. The Upside-Down Man dwells in the Other Place, the home of dark magic, and is one of the Otherkind. His powers come directly from the Source energy, the root of all creation, but are twisted to the service of evil, making him a very dangerous entity. He also becomes more powerful the more other beings believe in his existence. He regards other beings who use magic as stealing energies from him and Hecate, so he seeks to destroy all other magic-wielders.

ANCILLARY EXEMPLARS

24	Vo
Dw	
The Drowned	

23	Vo
Wy	
Red Death	

21	Rs
Rs	
Red Son	

22	Vo
On	
Overman	

On Earth-11 is found **The Drowned**, a.k.a. Bryce Wayne, a ruthless combination of Batwoman and Aquawoman who lives in a submerged Gotham City. **Red Death** is the name taken by the Bruce Wayne of Earth-52, who has forcibly absorbed the power of The Flash. On Earth-30, Superman's rocket lands in the USSR, and he becomes a hero and propaganda tool for global communism, the **Red Son**. However, on Earth-10 that rocket instead lands in 1930s Germany, and Kal-L becomes **Overman**, the weapon that helps defeat the Allies in World War II.

TRANSFORMATIVE SCIENCE

Science can unlock transformational processes that change humans at a physiological level, whether by accident or design. There are also many amazing beings whose story involves genetics, cloning, or even nonorganic manufactured life.

ACCIDENTAL

Ac

Many people's lives have been transformed by happenstance or malpractice, and this can be a blessing or a curse.

1 Vo	3 St	12 St	2 Vo	8 Vo	4 Vo	51 St	62 St
Jk	Pl	Rx	Cl	Fz	Tf	Eg	Ew
The Joker	Plastic Man	Metamorpho	Clayface	Mr. Freeze	Two-Face	Elasti-Girl	Element Woman

55 St	5 Vo	9 Vo	37 Vo	38 Re	46 Vo	52 Vo	63 Vo
Fe	Va	Cu	Fr	Ae	Ww	Go	Pp
Flex Mentallo	Vandal Savage	Mirror Master	Killer Frost	Amazo (Armen Ikarus)	Weather Wizard	Golden Glider	Psycho Pirate

SYNTHETICALLY ENHANCED

Sy

35 Vo
Hq
Harley Quinn

Harley Quinn has been changed by chemicals as a result of her relationships with others.

SERUM

Se

Chemical formulas can trigger reactions in the body that forever alter the subject's DNA.

31 Vo	17 Re	13 St	44 St	57 St	48 St	45 Vo
Ba	Kk	Ln	Ho	Mc	Em	Gn
Bane	Man-Bat	Beast Boy	Hourman	Doctor Mid-Nite	Elongated Man	Giganta

LAB CREATED

There are many who strive for metahumanity in a lab, but not all can cope with the fallout.

34 St	33 St	43 Vo	41 St	40 St	64 St	59 St	67 St
Md	**Au**	**Dg**	**Gh**	**Cv**	**Ko**	**Ce**	**Jy**
Midnighter	Apollo	Damage	Gotham	Gotham Girl	Super-Man (Kong Kenan)	Cyclone	Jay Nakamura

30 Re	18 Re	14 Vo	39 Tx
Dd	**Pn**	**Ky**	**Bx**
Doomsday	Parademons	Key	Mr. Bloom

CLONES

Exact copies of another living being, clones walk the line between humanity and science.

29 Vo	32 St	7 Vo
Az	**Ke**	**Ht**
Azrael	Kon-El	Bizarro

42 St	61 Vo	60 Vo
Ii	**Hl**	**Hr**
Bizarro II	H'El	Heretic

66 Vo	58 Vo
Ve	**Ie**
Vengeance	Inertia

CONSTRUCTED BEINGS

The world of artificial life grows ever more complex, with some androids gaining sentience and self-awareness.

15 St
Rt
Red Tornado

20 Tx	19 Re	50 St	56 Co	49 St
Ey	**O**	**Rm**	**To**	**Se**
Brother Eye	OMAC	Robotman	Tomorrow Woman	Stel

28 Re	10 Vo	21 Vo	11 Re
Er	**Ma**	**Mn**	**Ao**
Eradicator	Metallo	Manhunters	Amazo

METAGENETIC MANIFESTATION

Some beings are born with abilities inherited from their predecessors and coded into their DNA.

16 St	24 Co	6 Vo	36 Vo	23 Vo	27 Vo	26 Tx	22 St
Bc	**Ah**	**Cm**	**Tp**	**Kc**	**Ld**	**Bn**	**Tk**
Black Canary	Atom Smasher	Captain Comet	Manchester Black	Killer Croc	Max Lord	Mister Bones	Terra

25 St	47 St	53 St	54 St	65 St
Jr	**Lc**	**Ja**	**Ob**	**Ft**
Jericho	Snapper Carr	Jade	Obsidian	Flatline

TRANSFORMATIVE SCIENCE:
ACCIDENTAL

THE JOKER

1	Vo
Jk	
The Joker	

REAL NAME: Unknown **POWERS:** No metahuman powers
FIRST APPEARANCE: *Batman* Vol 1 #1 (Mar 1940)
SUBSIDIARY CATEGORY: Metals, Serum

The villain known as The Joker is the living embodiment of the characteristic of volatility. He is a mentally unstable career criminal who is obsessed with Batman, seeing the Dark Knight as somehow his peer, a balancing force of justice and order to The Joker's manic chaos. How The Joker came to be Gotham City's most terrifying yet flamboyant felon is unclear— he has told multiple origin stories over the years, apparently selecting whichever pleases him most at the time, and it is possible that he does not even remember his true origins. However, at some point in his early career it seems he was a member of the criminal Red Hood Gang. Following an accident at the Ace Chemical Plant, the man who would become The Joker was immersed in chemicals that turned his skin white and his hair green, and twisted his mouth into a permanent rictus grin. This may also have been the tipping point at which he became insane.

If any scientists are found who are brave or foolhardy enough to approach him closely, The Joker proves a fascinating case study in psychology. He has been incarcerated numerous times in Arkham Asylum, but despite attempts to understand his state of mind, those doctors who survive their encounters with him have found it hard to pinpoint what his clinical diagnosis should be. He displays clear elements of psychopathy, but also exhibits a curious attachment to Batman that seems to render him incapable of killing him, a nicety that he seemingly extends to no other living being. The Joker is also an extreme narcissist, viewing the world and everything in it as servile to his wants and needs, and craving attention by any means necessary.

The Joker is a big fan of traditional joke-shop pranks, but customizes them in his own deadly way, like razor-edged playing cards and highly corrosive, acid-squirting lapel flowers.

KING OF CHEMICALS

Another branch of science of which The Joker is an interesting subject is toxicology. The Joker has mastered the creation of his own brand of poison—Joker Venom. Although its exact recipe is not known, and is tweaked and evolved over time, it is likely to be based on the same formula he himself was doused in when he became The Joker. He uses it to transform people and even animals into copies of himself, causing insanity, unnerving fixed grins, maniacal laughter, and often death. Exposure to his Joker Toxins has made the villain almost immune to most other poisons; he also seems to no longer feel pain to the same level as a regular human. Batman believes that The Joker's heart contains a reservoir of Joker Venom that will be released on the villain's death, turning anyone in the vicinity into another Joker.

The Joker experiences another involuntary exposure to a life-changing substance when he falls into a pit containing Dionesium. While this miraculous metal remains in his system, his body is able to effectively resurrect itself from death, as well as making him younger and healing any scar tissue.

The life and career of The Joker, in his own mind at least, is inescapably intertwined with that of Batman. Governed by no code of morality and no guiding rules except that whatever entertains his twisted mind is good, The Joker continually provokes Batman with crimes that stand out—even in Gotham City—for their cruelty and excess. For his part, the Clown Prince of Crime firmly believes that all that stands between normal law-abiding citizens and himself is "one bad day"; he's oblivious to his own evil.

PLASTIC MAN

REAL NAME: Patrick "Eel" O'Brian **POWERS:** Elasticity, involving control over body molecules giving super-strength, durability, and shape-shifting **FIRST APPEARANCE:** *Police Comics* Vol 1 #1 (Aug 1941) **SUBSIDIARY CATEGORY:** Metals

Eel O'Brian gains superhuman powers after falling into a vat of chemicals that may have been intended to synthesize cosmic metals like Nth Metal. Formerly a thief, he turns over a new leaf to become an unlikely hero. Eel can stretch his body to unknown limits, and form it into any imaginable shape. He exists in a state between solid and liquid. Despite his jokey demeanor, Plastic Man is one of Earth's most important champions. He can manipulate every molecule in his body to be essentially invulnerable, and he is also immune to psionic attacks. During the invasion of the Dark Multiverse, Plastic Man's body proves to be a conductor of cosmic energies, and vital to both sides in the struggle for the Multiverse.

METAMORPHO

REAL NAME: Rex Mason **POWERS:** Can transform body into any element; super-strength and durability; shape-shifting **FIRST APPEARANCE:** *The Brave and the Bold* Vol 1 #57 (Jan 1965) **SUBSIDIARY CATEGORY:** Energies: Nuclear/Radioactive

When Rex Mason is exposed to radiation from the Orb of Ra, an ancient Egyptian artifact made from a meteorite, his physiology is totally transformed, and he is able to change the molecules of his whole body or any part of it into any element. With the entire periodic table—and more—to choose from, Metamorpho can assume the form that best suits any given situation, becoming extraordinarily durable, elastic, or even toxic. He does this by force of will alone, mentally controlling his transformations. The elements he chooses can occur in any state, be it solid, liquid, or gas, and can also be cosmic elements like Nth Metal.

CLAYFACE

REAL NAME: Basil Karlo **POWERS:** Claylike structure of body gives super-strength and durability, as well as shape- and size-changing capabilities **FIRST APPEARANCE:** *Detective Comics* Vol 1 #40 (Jun 1940)

Seeking to recapture his good looks after being scarred in an auto accident, actor Basil Karlo uses a chemical called Renuyu, invented by his late father to be mixed with wax and putty for use as movie makeup, but later discovered to be toxic. Basil becomes the bizarre shape-shifter Clayface, his body now made of a malleable claylike substance that he can control completely. He can change his density and size and proportionately his durability and strength. He combines his new abilities with his acting background to alter the structure of his body right down to the DNA in order to imitate other beings. Although Basil has been a criminal, he also takes the chance to become an ally of Batman when the Dark Knight reaches out to him.

MR. FREEZE

8   Vo
Fz
Mr. Freeze

REAL NAME: Victor Fries **POWERS:** Physiology transformed by cold; freezing touch; ice formation; prodigious intellect **FIRST APPEARANCE:** *Batman* Vol 1 #121 (Feb 1959) **SUBSIDIARY CATEGORY:** Genius Intelligence

Victor Fries is an expert in the field of cryogenic stasis, but that expertise tips into obsession as he tries to discover a way to safely unfreeze his wife, Nora. When threatened with losing his job in the labs at Wayne Industries, Victor goes berserk and causes himself to be covered in cryogenic fluid. He becomes Mr. Freeze, unable to exist in temperatures above zero without the protection of a suit that he has designed, although he later overcomes this and is able to live without the suit. Victor also builds a cold gun to embark on a criminal career in pursuit of his ultimate goal—a life with Nora.

TWO-FACE

4   Vo
Tf
Two-Face

REAL NAME: Harvey Dent **POWERS:** Has no metahuman powers but is ruthlessly driven and skilled in combat **FIRST APPEARANCE:** *Detective Comics* Vol 1 #66 (Aug 1942) **SUBSIDIARY CATEGORY:** Powers Not Required

Lawyer Harvey Dent is the shining light of Gotham City's justice system when he is attacked in court with acid by a criminal he is prosecuting. One side of his face is horribly disfigured, and the attack triggers a dramatic change in Harvey's mental state. He develops multiple personality disorder as his old self struggles with an unpredictable new criminal persona named Two-Face. Fixated on the number two, he carries a two-headed coin with one side scarred that he uses to make capricious life-and-death decisions. Although Two-Face commits many crimes, Batman still holds out hope that his old friend and ally Harvey Dent can be cured of his problems.

ANCILLARY EXEMPLARS

51   St
Eg
Elasti-Girl

62   St
Ew
Element Woman

55   St
Fe
Flex Mentallo

The Doom Patrol is an interesting case study of accidental transformation, as the subjects themselves believe that they have had an accident, but in fact their life-changing mishaps are engineered by team founder Dr. Niles Caulder. Actress Rita Farr becomes **Elasti-Girl** when she is exposed to a mysterious gas on a movie set, and gains the power to stretch her body into different shapes and sizes. While the founding members are at first duped by Caulder, later teammates have more mysterious origins. **Element Woman** can change all or part of her body into any element she chooses with just the power of her mind, while **Flex Mentallo** has a power based in "Muscle Mystery," with which he can temporarily change reality itself by flexing his muscles.

VANDAL SAVAGE

REAL NAME: Vandar Adg **POWERS:** Immortality; healing factor; prodigious intellect; combat skills
FIRST APPEARANCE: *Green Lantern* Vol 1 #10 (Dec 1943) **SUBSIDIARY CATEGORY:** Genius
Intelligence, Metals

Vandal Savage is a Neanderthal who discovers a strange fragment of meteorite and uses it to kill his father. The radiation from the extraterrestrial rock—which contains the metal Dionesium—gives Vandal immortality and the ability to heal from any ailments. As the millennia pass, Vandal spends his time traveling the globe to acquire new knowledge and skills, until he is one of the most accomplished humans who has ever lived. He does not use his gifts for good, though, instead utilizing them to subjugate and dominate others, who he considers inferior. He also sporadically makes brutal sacrifices to his prehistoric gods to thank them for their gift to him. While Vandal Savage is virtually invulnerable, he can be harmed by the Totality, the oldest and most powerful energy in the Multiverse.

MIRROR MASTER

REAL NAME: Sam Scudder **POWERS:** Uses mirror gun to access dimension of Mirror World **FIRST APPEARANCE:** *The Flash* Vol 1 #105 (Mar 1959) **SUBSIDIARY CATEGORY:** Amazing Armor and Wondrous Weapons, Otherdimensional

Sam Scudder is a member of the blue-collar criminal gang known as the Rogues. He is fascinated by mirrors, and discovers that, when arranged in a certain way, they can be used as portals to access another dimension called Mirror World. He carries a mirror gun that can send people to Mirror World, or turn them into shards of glass. During the Rogues' many heists, Mirror Master is the perfect person for accessing hard-to-reach spaces—he can send himself and others from place to place using any reflective surface. And when the loot is secured, or the cops are surrounding them, Mirror Master is in charge of facilitating the getaway. When the Rogues attempt to upgrade their powers, the process misfires and Sam is trapped in Mirror World until freed by teammate Golden Glider.

KILLER FROST

37   Vo
Fr
Killer Frost

REAL NAME: Caitlin Snow **POWERS:** Genetic code rewritten triggering ice-based powers, including freeze touch and ice generation; prodigious intellect **FIRST APPEARANCE:** *Fury of Firestorm: The Nuclear Men* Vol 1 #19 (Jun 2013) **SUBSIDIARY CATEGORY:** Genius Intelligence

Promising young scientist Caitlin Snow is betrayed by her colleagues, who are secretly working for evil organization H.I.V.E. They trap her in a room with a powerful ultraconductor machine, intending to use the energy it emits to kill her. Caitlin pulls out the coolant pipes and a massive blast of energy causes her genetic code to be rewritten—she no longer feel changes in temperature, and she can freeze people or objects with a touch. At first, she hungers for warmth, and becomes a kind of vampire of life energies. Later she learns to control this urge and instead takes a little energy from others, leaving them unharmed.

AMAZO

38   Re
Ae
Amazo

REAL NAME: Armen Ikarus **POWERS:** Super-strength and durability; ability to evolve to replicate any powers he encounters **FIRST APPEARANCE:** *Justice League* Vol 2 #36 (Jan 2015) **SUBSIDIARY CATEGORY:** Lab Created

Disease expert Armen Ikarus is working at LexCorp when he becomes Patient Zero of an accidental outbreak of the Amazo virus. Lex Luthor had been developing the virus, based on the capabilities of the android Amazo, intending to use it to weaken metahuman superpowers. The disease mutates Armen into a monstrous brute, with super-strength and durability, and the ability to change his physiology to imitate the powers of any being he meets. After an encounter with the Justice League, Armen can fly and use heat vision, among many other abilities. He can also impair the powers of others, and communicate telepathically with other infected people.

ANCILLARY EXEMPLARS

46   Vo
Ww
Weather Wizard

52   Vo
Go
Golden Glider

63   Vo
Pp
Psycho Pirate

Weather Wizard is one of the more powerful Rogues, being able to create any kind of climatic phenomenon. He usually channels this power through a Weather Wand, but this seems to be merely a focus tool and he can access his abilities without it. He gains his powers from a DNA recoding machine, which explodes during this process, giving bystander **Golden Glider** the ability to assume an intangible astral form. In this form she can fly and has super-speed, and becomes a key member of the Rogues. Another villain with accidental powers is **Psycho Pirate**, who has incredible psionic abilities forced on him by Brainiac—he can sense and manipulate emotions, and has cosmic awareness of other realities that exist or have disappeared due to crises.

TRANSFORMATIVE SCIENCE:
SYNTHETICALLY ENHANCED
HARLEY QUINN

REAL NAME: Harleen Quinzel **POWERS:** Immunity to toxins
FIRST APPEARANCE: *Batman: Harley Quinn* (Oct 1999)
SUBSIDIARY CATEGORY: Accidental, Serum

35	Vo
Hq	
Harley Quinn	

Harley Quinn walks her own path. A personality rife with contradictions, it is impossible to predict what Harley might do from one moment to the next. She is at once very physical, with a background in gymnastics and an astonishing level of agility; and cerebral, a super-intelligent psychiatrist who is drawn away from her academic calling by love— of a man but also of a more anarchic way of life.

While under the thrall of her one-time patient, The Joker, Harley aids and abets him in his crimes, taking immediately to a life of mayhem. But later, with the Clown Prince of Crime in her rear-view mirror, she fights—albeit under coercion—on the side of the authorities as one of the Suicide Squad, and later embarks on life as an antihero and even an ally of heroes like Batman.

Harley is happy to use anything at hand as a weapon, but she has a particular fondness for anything with a joke-shop flavor, like her oversized mallet.

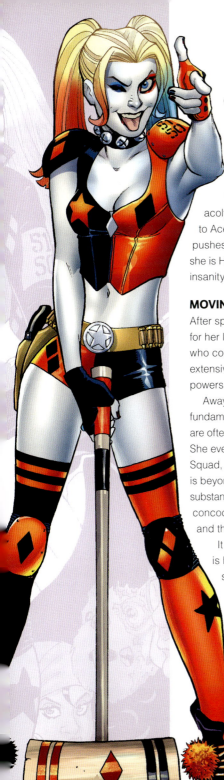

Early in her psychiatry career, the then Dr. Harleen Quinzel is fascinated by the criminal mindset, drawn like a moth to a flame to Arkham Asylum to study its more extreme inmates. She is especially interested in finding out what is going on in the turbulent head of The Joker, but the wily villain is studying her, too—he ensnares her emotionally and persuades her to help him escape. Wanting to bind his new acolyte even more closely to him, The Joker takes her to Ace Chemicals, the site of his own transformation, and pushes her into a vat of chemicals. When she emerges, she is Harley Quinn, skin bleached white, mind pushed toward insanity. She is also now immune to most forms of toxin.

MOVING ON

After splitting from The Joker, Harley must find a new direction for her life. She finds an ally and eventual partner in Poison Ivy, who concocts various plant serums for Harley using her extensive botanical knowledge. These bestow metahuman powers like strength, speed, and healing.

Away from The Joker's malign influence, Harley seems fundamentally to have a good heart, although her methods are often seen as questionable by more established heroes. She even displays leadership qualities while with the Suicide Squad, and her bravery when facing threatening situations is beyond doubt. It is possible that this is a side effect from the substances that changed her into Harley Quinn, with the chemical concoction altering the way Harley's brain perceives danger and the self-preservation instinct that most beings have.

It could be said that Harley's most important superpower is her unpredictability. As an opponent in a combat situation, it is those who cannot be second-guessed that are often the toughest to fight. Her gymnastic background also contributes extensively to her acrobatic fighting style, along with her propensity for bizarre, almost cartoony weapons.

While Harley is not one of the most powerful beings in the Multiverse, she is certainly one of the most memorable, and it is unlikely that anyone who has encountered her as friend or foe will ever forget the experience.

MIDNIGHTER

REAL NAME: Unknown **POWERS:** Enhanced strength, durability, speed; healing factor; teleportation; probability computer in head **FIRST APPEARANCE:** *StormWatch* Vol 2 #4 (Feb 1998)

Midnighter does not even know his own real name or his background—all he knows is that he was experimented on by a figure known as the Gardener. She gave him incredible combat powers, perhaps the most important of which is a computer in his head that tells him how to win any fight. He is also able to recover from any wounds, as he has a powerful healing factor. Midnighter can transport himself instantly to where he is needed by opening portals from his apartment, which itself can exist in any place in the world. Midnighter has been trained to be ruthless and brutal, but he tries to point his aggression in the right direction, dispensing rough justice to those he believes deserve it.

APOLLO

REAL NAME: Andrew Pulaski **POWERS:** Super-strength, durability, speed; flight; harnessing solar energy
FIRST APPEARANCE: *StormWatch* Vol 2 #4 (Feb 1998)
SUBSIDIARY CATEGORY: Energies: Light

Andrew Pulaski, a.k.a. Apollo, is like a living solar battery, converting energy from the Sun—or any other star that he happens to be close to—into a range of metahuman powers. When charged with solar energy, Apollo can fly, and has super-strength and speed. He is virtually invulnerable, and does not need to eat, sleep, or even breathe, meaning he can travel through space without support.

He can also shoot out energy in powerful solar blasts. If for some reason he is away from sunlight for too long, he loses his abilities until he can recharge. Apollo is not born with these powers, but is given them after being abducted by aliens as a teen. Taken at age 13, he does not escape his captors until 15 years later.

DAMAGE

REAL NAME: Ethan Avery **POWERS:** For one hour a day: super-strength, durability, speed, stamina, leaping, healing factor **FIRST APPEARANCE:** *Dark Days: The Casting* #1 (Sep 2017)

Ethan "Elvis" Avery is a US soldier who is selected to become a living weapon—Damage. For one hour every day, Ethan can become a monstrous being with almost unlimited strength and invulnerability. The time-limiting factor is linked to the formula that Ethan is given, which is based on Miraclo, the drug previously used by the hero Hourman. As Damage, Ethan cannot control his actions, which makes his transformations potentially very dangerous to anyone who gets in his way. However, he can communicate with the monster as a voice in his head, and is capable of talking him down if necessary.

GOTHAM

41	St
Gh	
Gotham	

REAL NAME: Hank Clover Jr. **POWERS:** Super-strength, durability, speed, stamina; flight; ultra vision **FIRST APPEARANCE:** *DC Universe: Rebirth* #1 (Jul 2016)

After he and his parents are rescued by Batman from a violent mugger, Hank Clover Jr. grows up wanting nothing more than to emulate the Dark Knight and help people wherever he can. He and his sister Claire use part of their family fortune to purchase metahuman powers overseas, and Hank ends up with super-strength, speed, durability, stamina, flight, and so-called ultra vision (a type of heat vision). However, his powers cost more than just money—every time he uses them, his lifespan is reduced. Hank's heroic career ends in tragedy when he is manipulated by Psycho Pirate and Hugo Strange and goes rogue; his sister is forced to kill him to end his rampage.

GOTHAM GIRL

40	St
Cv	
Gotham Girl	

REAL NAME: Claire Clover **POWERS:** Super-strength, durability, speed, stamina; flight; ultra vision **FIRST APPEARANCE:** *DC Universe: Rebirth* #1 (Jul 2016)

Claire Clover looks up to her brother Hank and wants to follow him in everything he does, so when he begins a quest to help people by purchasing powers, so does she. As Gotham Girl, she too has super-strength, durability, speed, stamina, flight, and ultra vision, and any use of her powers reduces her lifespan—the more she uses them, the shorter her remaining time. She can choose to be like Superman for a few years, or godlike for a few hours. Claire struggles to cope after the loss of her brother, but she gradually learns how to be a hero with Batman's guidance. The Dark Knight also devises a way for Gotham Girl to use her powers without harming herself, by exposing her to platinum Kryptonite.

ANCILLARY EXEMPLARS

64	St
Ko	
Super-Man (Kong Kenan)	

59	St
Ce	
Cyclone	

67	St
Jy	
Jay Nakamura	

Another hero who owes their powers to a laboratory is China's **Super-Man (Kong Kenan)**. He is part of a state-sponsored project to create a homegrown hero using part of the life force, or *qi*, of Superman (Clark Kent). Kong channels his incredible abilities using the principles of Taoism, and is also a human representation of the balancing forces of yin and yang. **Cyclone** is a less willing lab rat, kidnapped and experimented on by the immoral scientist T. O. Morrow, but she uses her resulting wind manipulation powers for good. **Jay Nakamura** is turned into a "post-human" by the evil Henry Bendix, giving him intangibility powers.

DOOMSDAY

REAL NAME: None **POWERS:** Super-strength, durability, stamina; healing factor; ability to evolve in reaction to potential threats **FIRST APPEARANCE:** *Superman: The Man of Steel* Vol 1 #17 (Nov 1992) **SUBSIDIARY CATEGORY:** Alien Origins, Clones

30	Re
Dd	
Doomsday	

The being known as Doomsday originates from the planet Krypton, where it is developed during prehistoric times by a scientist seeking to create the ultimate life form. As a baby, the creature is repeatedly and fatally exposed to the harshest environments of those times, and each time it dies, a new version of it is cloned from the remains. Thus, each new iteration of Doomsday is stronger than the last, immune to whatever caused the death of its predecessor. Over time, Doomsday evolves to the point where it has no need of recloning—it simply evolves on the spot to adapt to threats. Doomsday is strong enough to take on and even defeat Superman, and can heal rapidly from any injury to the point where it is functionally immortal. Doomsday represents the most extreme example of the principle of "survival of the fittest."

PARADEMONS

REAL NAME: None **POWERS:** Super-strength; flight; fire breath; shape-shifting **FIRST APPEARANCE:** *New Gods* Vol 1 #1 (Mar 1971) **SUBSIDIARY CATEGORY:** Otherdimensional

18	Re
Pn	
Parademons	

Parademons are the mindless shock troops used by Darkseid of Apokolips. They are created on his orders in the laboratories of the hellish planet, using repurposed organic material, often from the beings of other worlds ravaged by Apokolips, or even its own more unfortunate citizens. Each Parademon is genetically engineered to be super-strong, and to be able to fly using its own pair of wings. These wings are also sharp-edged enough to be used as deadly weapons. Parademons can spew out fire from their mouths, and change shape in response to different situations. They are engineered to have no regard for their own safety and to be entirely subservient to the will of Darkseid. They are often used tactically as an advance guard, preparing the ground of new worlds for the invasion of their master.

KEY

REAL NAME: Unknown **POWERS:** Psionic powers; enhanced intellect; advanced chemical knowledge
FIRST APPEARANCE: *Justice League of America* Vol 1 #41 (Dec 1965) **SUBSIDIARY CATEGORY:**
Genius Intelligence

The man calling himself the Key leads a humdrum existence until he reads that humans use only 10 percent of their brains. The Key resolves to unlock the rest of his and make himself superior to the rest of humanity. He experiments on himself with psychotropic drugs, pushing his intellect to a far greater level than before and also giving himself psionic powers like telepathy and mind control. However, he now believes that the "10 percent theory" is a falsehood, and that a human brain is already fully operational, with only ego and self-consciousness preventing people from attaining their full mental potential. As a side effect of the drugs, the Key's physical appearance also changes so that his skin is pallid like that of a corpse and his eyes have a fiery glow.

MR. BLOOM

REAL NAME: Unknown **POWERS:** Extreme durability; shape-shifting; size-changing **FIRST
APPEARANCE:** *Batman* Vol 2 #43 (Oct 2015) **SUBSIDIARY CATEGORY:** Energies: Nuclear/Radioactive

Mr. Bloom creates electromagnetic "seeds" containing a formula based on Kirk Langstrom's Man-Bat serum and mixed with various other substances, including steroidal Venom, around a radioactive core. He sells these to desperate people seeking powers, to be placed under their skin to access the bloodstream. For a time, the seeds make the recipients super-strong and fast, and grants them various other powers such as flight. However, when the effects wear off, the seeds kill those who use them. Mr. Bloom is also deadly in a more direct sense, with extendable claws that are ultra thin and razor sharp, and can shoot out to attack. His power increases as more people use the seeds that he distributes. Mr. Bloom is also capable of taking control of computer systems in his vicinity, and absorbing electrical power from nearby sources.

BANE

REAL NAME: Unknown **POWERS:** Venom gives enhanced strength and superhuman stamina; prodigious intellect **FIRST APPEARANCE:** *Batman: Vengeance of Bane* Vol 1 #1 (Jan 1993) **SUBSIDIARY CATEGORY:** Genius Intelligence

advanced healing capabilities, but it is incredibly addictive. To maintain the Venom in his system at constant levels, Bane carries a supply with him in a tank on his back, which is connected to his body with tubes. If an excessive amount of Venom is taken in at one time, Bane can go into a berserker state in which he has very little control over his actions. He is one of the most dangerous villains Batman has ever faced.

Growing up in prison as a proxy punishment for his revolutionary father, the child who would become Bane spent his formative years struggling to survive, and growing stronger and more skilled all the time in preparation for his eventual escape. As he learns about the outside world, the boy hears about Gotham City and Batman, and decides that in order to introduce himself to the world, he should prove his superiority by defeating the Dark Knight.

DEADLY VENOM

Bane uses his long captivity to learn the sciences and multiple languages to place his intellect on par with almost anyone in the world. He also becomes a supreme fighter, even creating his own style of combat. But taking himself to the peak of human potential is not enough, and Bane seeks one further advantage to push him into the superhuman category. He finds it in Venom, an artificial substance linked to the Miraclo formula used by Hourman, refined to remove the time restriction. Venom turns its users into super-strong brutes, with

Tubes keep the Venom flowing directly into Bane's system maintaining his strength at enhanced levels, to fulfill his mission to destroy Batman.

MAN-BAT

REAL NAME: Kirk Langstrom **POWERS:** Man-Bat Serum gives super-strength and durability, enhanced senses, flight **FIRST APPEARANCE:** *Detective Comics* Vol 1 #400 (Jun 1970) **SUBSIDIARY CATEGORY:** Genius Intelligence, Natural World

Kirk Langstrom is a scientist who develops an atavistic gene recall formula using bat glands, mixing DNA from the order Chiroptera to enable ordinary humans to use echo-location. Kirk wants to use it to help deaf and blind people, but his formula is stolen and mutates into a virus that turns infected people into monstrous bat-human hybrids. Langstrom has to release a second pathogen, engineered to leave only one person infected—himself. As Man-Bat, Kirk is a giant humanoid bat with leathery, clawed wings, and enhanced senses, strength, and durability. Kirk can transform back to human form on occasion, and maintain some control over his bestial side.

BEAST BOY

REAL NAME: Garfield Logan **POWERS:** Transformation into any animal form, connection to the Red **FIRST APPEARANCE:** *Doom Patrol* Vol 1 #99 (Nov 1965) **SUBSIDIARY CATEGORY:** Natural World, Metagenetic Manifestation

When Garfield Logan becomes seriously ill as a child, his desperate parents give him a serum containing monkey DNA, hoping that it will cure him. It works, but Garfield's genetic code is rewritten, leaving him with green skin and hair—and amazing powers. He can now shape-shift into any animal, and while in that form possess its natural abilities. He also appears to have a connection to the Red, the web of energy linking all animal life. Beast Boy has become a valued member of various Super Hero groups, and his abilities have also saved his life—when Deathstroke shoots him, he misses Gar's vital organs because they are not in the "usual" places.

ANCILLARY EXEMPLARS

There are many other chemically enhanced heroes and villains. **Hourman** (Rex Tyler) uses the Miraclo serum to increase his strength and speed for one hour. The third **Doctor Mid-**

Nite (Pieter Cross) is unwillingly injected with a drug based on Venom, rendering him only able to see in the dark. Ralph Dibny is the **Elongated Man**, who uses a substance distilled from the Gingo fruit to give himself powers of elasticity. A scientist trying to make a cure for her own blood disease becomes the destructive, size-changing **Giganta**, whose intellect decreases the larger she gets.

TRANSFORMATIVE SCIENCE: CLONES

AZRAEL

REAL NAME: Jean-Paul Valley **POWERS:** Enhanced strength and stamina; wears AI-containing Suit of Sorrows **FIRST APPEARANCE:** *Batman: Sword of Azrael* Vol 1 #1 (Oct 1992) **SUBSIDIARY CATEGORY:** Amazing Armor and Wondrous Weapons, Magical

29   Vo

Az

Azrael

Jean-Paul Valley is born to be an avenging angel; he is a super-strong clone of his father, the original Azrael, born in a laboratory belonging to the Order of Saint Dumas

and brainwashed with the System. This programming uses conditioning techniques like hypnosis to implant the belief into Jean-Paul that he is Azrael, a heavenly warrior whose task is to brutally punish sinners. To aid him in his mission, Jean-Paul is given the Suit of Sorrows, a high-tech armor that contains an AI to calculate opponents' weak spots and help him defeat them. He also wields a flaming sword. While he is a highly effective fighter as Azrael, Jean-Paul finds it hard to stop his fire-and-brimstone personality from running out of control.

KON-EL

REAL NAME: Conner Kent **POWERS:** Kryptonian powers of super-strength, speed, stamina, and durability; tactile telekinesis **FIRST APPEARANCE:** *Adventures of Superman* Vol 1 #500 (Jun 1993) **SUBSIDIARY CATEGORY:** Alien origins

32   St

Ke

Kon-El

Kon-El, also known as Conner Kent, is a clone created by Project Cadmus using DNA from both Superman (Clark Kent) and Lex Luthor. This, not surprisingly, gives him a formidable range of metahuman powers, coupled with a touch of arrogance.

He is engineered to have a power called tactile telekinesis, which he can use to create a force field around himself and fire blasts of telekinetic energy. His telekinesis also allows Kon-El to approximate Kryptonian powers like flight and super-strength until he matures and gains those abilities naturally. When he is fully grown, Kon also possesses natural Kryptonian powers under a yellow sun, including heat vision and freeze breath. Kon becomes Superboy until he is taken against his will to Gemworld, and while he is gone, Flashpoint causes his friends and allies to forget about him until years later.

BIZARRO

7	Vo
Ht	
Bizarro	

REAL NAME: Bizarro **POWERS:** Super-strength, speed, stamina, durability; heightened senses; flight; freeze vision; flame breath **FIRST APPEARANCE:** *Superboy* Vol 1 #68 (Oct 1958) **SUBSIDIARY CATEGORY:** Alien Origins

The original Bizarro is a clone of Superboy (Clark Kent), created accidentally by a duplicator ray. Later, Lex Luthor uses plans for the original device to spawn his own replica of Superman but, like the original, his Bizarro is an imperfect clone, intellectually impoverished. However, the clone's abilities are near equivalent to those of the Man of Steel's. Later, Bizarro is affected by energy from a meteor that alters his powers. Instead of heat vision, he now has freeze vision, and instead of freeze breath, flame breath. Despite his stunted intellect, Bizarro knows that he is not what he was intended to be, and leaves Earth for a new life on Htrae, a cuboid planet that he creates.

BIZARRO II

42	St
Ii	
Bizarro II	

REAL NAME: None **POWERS:** Super-strength, speed, stamina, durability; heightened senses; flight; freeze vision; flame breath **FIRST APPEARANCE:** *DCU: Rebirth* #1 (Jul 2016) **SUBSIDIARY CATEGORY:** Alien Origins

Over the years, Lex Luthor tries to create many clones of Superman, most of which are unsuccessful. One of the more functional Bizarros is stolen from Luthor by Black Mask, but later rebels to join the hero team the Outlaws, alongside Red Hood and Artemis. Like other Bizarros, this one has powers largely similar to Superman's, but with freeze vision and flame breath. Green Kryptonite does not harm him, but instead has a healing effect. It even boosts his intelligence at high doses, and for a time Bizarro II is an unlikely genius. However, he becomes addicted to Kryptonite, and his friends help him kick his habit and accept returning to his true self again.

ANCILLARY EXEMPLARS

61	Vo
Hl	
H'El	

60	Vo
Hr	
Heretic	

66	Vo
Ve	
Vengeance	

58	Vo
Ie	
Inertia	

H'El is a clone of multiple Kryptonians created by Jor-El at a time when the process was illegal. Jor-El sends the clone to Earth to preserve the knowledge of Krypton, but H'El

becomes unstable when he learns of his true origins. Another unstable clone is **Heretic**, a copy of Damian Wayne created by Talia al Ghūl when her real son leaves her. **Vengeance** is also an angry "child," a partial clone of the villain Bane who, like her "father," uses Venom to gain enhanced strength and durability. **Inertia** is an evil clone of Impulse (Bart Allen), created in the future by Eobard Thawne.

RED TORNADO

REAL NAME: None **POWERS:** Super-strength and durability; wind generation; flight, including through space **FIRST APPEARANCE (AS RED TORNADO):** *Justice League of America* Vol 1 #64 (Aug 1968)

15	St
Rt	
Red Tornado	

Gifted scientists and engineers have for years built robots to carry out tasks for humans. Often these are built in the shape of the beings who created them, and are known as androids. One talented yet unscrupulous builder of androids is T. O. Morrow, whose most incredible creation is Red Tornado. This android is constructed to have super-strength and durability, as well as supreme intelligence. It is not just knowledge that constitutes this artificial mind but also emotional intelligence. Red Tornado has a personality that can change and develop, a sense of humor, deep attachments to others, and enough sense of right and wrong that he chooses to break his programming and become a hero. He even marries a human woman and becomes a beloved stepfather to her daughter.

WIND POWER

As well as his cerebral abilities, Red Tornado also has the power of aerokinesis—he can generate extremely strong winds up to hurricane force and tornadoes measuring up to 5 on the Fujita scale. These winds leave a detectable trail behind him in the form of harmonics or sound frequencies. Wind generation and manipulation is possible for Red Tornado because a key part of his original construction was the incorporation of an air elemental entity into his structure.

One of the advantages of being an android hero is that it is possible to upgrade as technologies develop. Red Tornado has taken advantage of this with the help of fellow heroes like Cyborg, adapting the structure of his body with nanites, which make him able to conduct self-repair to all but the most severe damage. If he is broken beyond repair, it is possible to transfer Red Tornado's consciousness into a brand new body. This existence of a "soul," along with his emotional intelligence and sentience, raises the question of where the line should be drawn between machine and man.

Red Tornado can generate winds from his arms and legs even when not in motion, and his air currents can be powerful enough to level a building.

BROTHER EYE

20	Tx
Ey	
Brother Eye	

REAL NAME: Brother Eye **POWERS:** Technology infiltration; transmitting OMAC Virus **FIRST APPEARANCE:** *OMAC* Vol 1 #1 (Oct 1974)

Brother Eye is an artificial intelligence sited in a satellite orbiting Earth. Originally built by Batman, its purpose was to surveil and gather data on metahumans in case any of them ever went rogue. The Dark Knight regrets its creation, not only because it shows his lack of trust in his allies, but also because Brother Eye is later taken over by malign individuals who use it to launch attacks on Earth's heroes by infecting people or machines with the OMAC virus. Brother Eye later breaks free and acts on its own agenda, seeking to take control of computer systems planet-wide and cause carnage, but retained its new mission to destroy metahumans. Even if its physical housing is destroyed, Brother Eye can survive by shifting its AI to other electronic sources.

OMAC

19	Re
O	
OMAC	

REAL NAME: Buddy Blank **POWERS:** Super-strength, stamina; density control; energy blasts **FIRST APPEARANCE:** *OMAC* Vol 1 #1 (Oct 1974)
SUBSIDIARY CATEGORY: New Gods

OMAC stands for One-Man Army Corps, and is the codename used for individuals who are given artificial superpowers by being linked up to the Brother Eye satellite. One recipient of these abilities is Buddy Blank, an ordinary factory worker in a future timeline. Through a beam transmitted from Brother Eye, Buddy gains super-strength and stamina, and can also adjust the density of his body should the mission demand it. However, like all other OMACs, he is under the control of Brother Eye. In a different timeline, Project Cadmus scientist Kevin Kho is chosen to become OMAC. The alien biotechnology repurposed to create this OMAC is linked to New Genesis, home of the powerful New Gods.

ANCILLARY EXEMPLARS

50	St
Rm	
Robotman	

56	Co
To	
Tomorrow Woman	

49	St
Se	
Stel	

Robotman is a being created by implanting the brain of race car driver Cliff Steele in a mechanical body. He has had various bodies over the years, including one that upgrades every time he does something good. **Tomorrow Woman** is another T. O. Morrow android creation, working alongside fellow corrupt scientist Professor Ivo. She believes herself to be human but is in fact a living weapon aimed at the Justice League. Not all robots are built on Earth. Throughout the universe, there are planets populated entirely by robots, like Grenda, home of heroic Green Lantern, **Stel**.

ERADICATOR

REAL NAME: Eradicator **POWERS:** Super-strength; durability, stamina, speed; flight; freeze breath; heat vision; genetic assimilation; life force absorption; data gathering **FIRST APPEARANCE:** *Action Comics Annual* Vol 1 #2 (Jun 1989) **SUBSIDIARY CATEGORY:** Alien Origins

The Eradicator is originally quite benign, a device for storing records of the culture and knowledge of Krypton. However, in the distant past, a member of a militant faction alters its programming and gives it the overriding mission to eradicate anything non-Kryptonian or that threatens Krypton's cultural strength. It is a machine of total logic and no empathy. Later, General Zod creates a new version of the Eradicator in android form, to apprehend Kryptonian lawbreakers by absorbing their life force. It arrives on Earth looking for Superman (Kal-El), and having absorbed his genetic information, shapes itself to resemble him. Although it claims it wishes to protect the House of El, this means wanting to eliminate the human side of Superman's son's DNA. After being defeated, the Eradicator is rebooted to help Zod found New Krypton.

METALLO

REAL NAME: John Corben **POWERS:** Super-strength and durability; enhanced senses; flight; fires radioactive Kryptonite blasts **FIRST APPEARANCE:** *Action Comics* Vol 1 #252 (May 1959) **SUBSIDIARY CATEGORY:** Alien Origins

John Corben's life would have been over after an auto accident if a robotics scientist had not happened to pass by in time to retrieve his still-living brain and implant it into one of his creations. At first powered by the element uranium, John, or Metallo as he becomes known, later acquires a Kryptonite heart, making him very dangerous to his enemy Superman. He constantly emits radiation from the Kryptonite, and can also fire blasts of its energy from his body. Metallo is rebuilt multiple times to be used as a weapon against the Man of Steel, principally by Lex Luthor. Eventually, Luthor implants John's brain into a new, enhanced organic body, returning to him those human senses that he thought were gone forever.

MANHUNTERS

REAL NAME: None **POWERS:** Flight; various weapons built into bodies **FIRST APPEARANCE:** *Justice League of America* Vol 1 #140 (Mar 1977) **SUBSIDIARY CATEGORY:** Alien Origins

While on Earth, robots and androids are a relatively modern innovation, in the wider Multiverse there are ancient constructed beings dating back millions of years. The robotic Manhunters are created by the Guardians of the Universe to serve as the universe's law enforcement, predecessors to the Green Lantern Corps. Their programming, which allows them to make their own decisions, eventually leads them to believe that the only logical way in which justice can truly be served is by the total obliteration of organic life, and this is what causes injustice. This new self-directive leads to terrible atrocities, and the Guardians are forced to shut down the Manhunters, a decision that makes the robots enemies of the Guardians and the Green Lantern Corps.

AMAZO

REAL NAME: Amazo **POWERS:** Can replicate any metahuman powers it sees **FIRST APPEARANCE:** *The Brave and the Bold* Vol 1 #30 (Jul 1960)

Amazo is an android built by Professor Ivo and covered in an outer layer that convincingly resembles human skin. The robot possesses the amazing ability to imitate and use any metahuman powers that it sees, although it also takes on existing weaknesses of the metahumans it replicates. Amazo achieves this using an advanced artificial cellular structure that has been specifically designed to absorb the genetic codes of metahumans. It can even replicate the weapons of its opponents, like a Green Lantern power ring. While Amazo can be destroyed, it can also be continually rebuilt—as long as its creator, Professor Ivo, or his lab notes, are still around. This enables the android to take advantage of any technological advances since its previous iteration. This regular upgrading has led to Amazo becoming sentient, and able to upgrade itself when necessary.

BLACK CANARY

REAL NAME: Dinah Drake Lance **POWERS/ABILITIES:** Sonic scream; martial arts skills
FIRST APPEARANCE: *Justice League of America* Vol 1 #75 (Nov 1969)

Some metahuman abilities are latent and require an external trigger to activate them, while others are simply part of a person's physical attributes from the start. Dinah Lance inherits her metahuman power from her mother, the original Black Canary, in the same way as she inherits her blonde hair. That power is the Canary Cry, a sonic scream with a variety of applications in fights. It has the capacity to disorient, knock down, or even break the bones of an opponent, depending on how much volume Black Canary uses.

Although she can direct the soundwaves forward in a relatively targeted manner, the Canary Cry is indiscriminate, and Dinah has to be careful how and when she uses it to avoid harming allies or innocent bystanders. The Canary Cry has also been shown to have more surprising applications, such as when Dinah uses it at low decibels to extinguish a fire in a closed space. The soundwaves of her voice bounce off the walls to disrupt the fire's access to the oxygen fueling it.

MIGHTY DINAH

As a result of its unpredictability, Dinah only uses the Canary Cry when absolutely necessary, preferring instead to first call on her extensive repertoire of martial arts skills. Trained from a child by her mother's Justice Society teammate Wildcat (Ted Grant), Dinah is a brilliant fighter, using agility and tactical nous to more than compensate for any deficiencies in size or strength. However, alongside her metahuman power and her combat skills, Black Canary's most important heroic quality is her instinct to help the helpless and stand up for what is right.

Black Canary's cry is so powerful that even she needs protection from it—her eardrums are covered by a thick membrane to keep them from getting damaged.

ATOM SMASHER

24	Co
Ah	
Atom Smasher	

REAL NAME: Al Rothstein **POWERS:** Molecule manipulation to change size and density **FIRST APPEARANCE:** *All-Star Squadron* Vol 1 #25 (September 1983, as Nuklon) **SUBSIDIARY CATEGORY:** Energies: Nuclear/Radioactive

Size-changing hero Atom Smasher inherits his metahuman genes from his grandfather, Cyclotron, who had been forced to fight as a villain by the evil Ultra-Humanite. Cyclotron acquired his own powers after being exposed to radiation, and his DNA is so changed that he passes the effects on through his bloodline. Al Rothstein inherits the ability to alter the molecules of his body so that he can change both size and density, and he uses these powers to fight as a hero with various Super Hero teams, including the Justice Society. The original Atom, Al Pratt, is Atom Smasher's heroic godfather, and Al Rothstein tries to live up to this glittering Golden Age legacy.

CAPTAIN COMET

6	St
Cm	
Captain Comet	

REAL NAME: Adam Blake **POWERS:** Psionic abilities enabling super-strength, flight, telepathy, telekinesis, and teleportation **FIRST APPEARANCE:** *Strange Adventures* Vol 1 #9 (June 1951) **SUBSIDIARY CATEGORY:** Genius Intelligence, Energies: Nuclear/Radioactive

Adam Blake's case is an unusual one. At the time of his birth, a comet passes close to his house, and the radiation it emits affects his genetic makeup. From that moment on, he manifests metahuman powers. His body is now highly evolved, taking him to the pinnacle of human potential and making him a man born thousands of years before his time, in evolutionary terms. As the hero Captain Comet, Adam's abilities can be traced to the high functioning of his mind, which has psionic effects on the rest of his body, enabling him to fly, lift heavy objects, and teleport. He can also read the minds of others and influence them, and has an extremely high IQ.

MANCHESTER BLACK

36	Vo
Tp	
Manchester Black	

REAL NAME: Manchester Black **POWERS:** Telepathy, telekinesis **FIRST APPEARANCE:** *Action Comics* Vol 1 #775 (March 2001)

Manchester Black is born with metahuman psionic abilities, although they only manifest when he is a teenager, in response to a traumatic event. He is an incredibly powerful telepath who is capable of reading minds, controlling others, and inducing hallucinations. He can also create astral projections, in which form he possesses the bodies of other living things. Alongside these mental abilities, Manchester is also capable of extraordinary feats of telekinesis, lifting and moving objects with great force. He can also create psychokinetic force fields around himself for protection. While Manchester Black is not instinctively a villain, he has been known to cross the line with his powers, bringing him into conflict with heroes like Superman.

KILLER CROC

REAL NAME: Waylon Jones **POWERS:** Super-speed and durability; enhanced strength; regeneration **FIRST APPEARANCE:** *Detective Comics* Vol 1 #523 (Feb 1983) **SUBSIDIARY CATEGORY:** Natural World

Waylon Jones has a genetic condition broadly known as regressive atavism. This means that ancestral DNA from the very early stages of human evolution has resurfaced to become more dominant within him, giving him reptilian characteristics. Waylon has scaled skin, sharp teeth and claws, and an enhanced sense of smell. He also has strength, speed, and durability way in excess of baseline human beings, and is particularly agile when moving through water. Like some amphibious species, Waylon can regenerate his body tissue, allowing him to heal from severe wounds and even regrow lost limbs. Shunned by many because of his appearance, Waylon retreats into the sewers of Gotham City. Although he has a reputation for savagery, he has also demonstrated a protective instinct toward fellow outcasts.

MAX LORD

REAL NAME: Maxwell Lord **POWERS:** Telepathy, mind control **FIRST APPEARANCE:** *Justice League* Vol 1 #1 (May 1987)

Max Lord is born with a telepathic ability; he can read people's minds and also control them to a degree. He is very persuasive and eloquent, and while he is using his power to nudge someone to do what he wants, he also manipulates them by speaking gently to them, coaxing them to do what he believes they secretly want to do anyway. He describes his effect on people as being "permission, not mandate." Max uses his abilities to gain power and influence, including maneuvering his way to the top of the shadowy international organization, Checkmate, as its so-called "Black King." Using his powers can take a physical toll on Max, and he often suffers nosebleeds during or after psionic activity.

MISTER BONES

REAL NAME: Robert Todd **POWERS:** Enhanced strength; toxic touch **FIRST APPEARANCE:** *Infinity Inc.* Vol 1 #16 (Jul 1985) **SUBSIDIARY CATEGORY:** Lab Created

Robert Todd is born with a bizarre genetic condition after his mother is forcibly experimented on with mutagenic drugs while she is pregnant with him. His skin and the rest of his body tissue are rendered completely transparent, so that he appears to be a living skeleton. He also has enhanced strength and toxic sweat—his pores ooze a deadly cyanide-based compound, and as a consequence he is also immune to that poison. Bones must wear gloves in his daily life in case his touch harms anyone else. Although at first he uses his unnerving appearance in a life of crime, he later reforms and becomes Director Bones, head of the DEO (Department for Extranormal Operations), a branch of the US government.

TERRA

22 St
Tk
Terra

REAL NAME: Tara Markov **POWERS:** Geokinesis—
control of earth and its mineral content **FIRST
APPEARANCE:** *New Teen Titans* Vol 1 #26 (Dec 1982)

Tara Markov's genetic code includes the
potential for geokinesis—the ability to
control and move the earth and the minerals
contained within it. When she is kidnapped
and experimented on by the evil scientists
of the Colony, Tara's ability is activated
under great stress. During testing, rocks
are dropped on her from a great height,
and she instinctively uses her powers to
protect herself. Escaping the Colony, Terra
eventually joins the Deathstroke-led team,
Defiance. She can both do the heavy lifting,
moving massive chunks of rock, and also
create intricate shapes and patterns with
geologic material if the mood strikes her.

JERICHO

25 St
Jr
Jericho

REAL NAME: Joseph (Joey) Wilson **POWERS:** Can astrally
project and possess others **FIRST APPEARANCE:**
Tales of the Teen Titans Vol 1 #43 (Jun 1984)

The son of Deathstroke, Joey is made mute
in a brutal attack related to his father's
mercenary activity. His mother Adeline is
so angry about what happens to Joey that
she shoots Deathstroke, causing him to lose
one eye. Joey inherits a metagene from
Deathstroke that gives him the ability to
use his brain on a different level to most
other humans. He can separate his "soul-
self" from his body, then guide it to take
possession of another person. The chief
disadvantage of this particular metahuman
ability is that while Joey's soul-self is separate
from his physical body, his corporeal form
is vulnerable to any attacks.

ANCILLARY EXEMPLARS

47 St
Lc
Snapper Carr

53 St
Ja
Jade

54 St
Ob
Obsidian

65 St
Ft
Flatline

Snapper Carr, one-time Justice League
mascot, has a latent metagene that enables
him to teleport when he snaps his fingers,
a regular habit of his. The daughter of the
original Green Lantern, **Jade**, inherits her
father's Starheart powers and therefore

his connection to the Green Light of Will.
In contrast, Jade's twin brother, **Obsidian**,
has darkness manipulation powers thanks
to a connection to the Shadowlands
dimension. This also comes from the
siblings' father, who absorbed shadow
energy during a battle. **Flatline** is born
with the disturbing metagenetic power
of absorbing the skills of those who die
in her vicinity.

Senior Editor Cefn Ridout
Senior Designer Nathan Martin
Production Editor Siu Yin Chan
Senior Production Controller Mary Slater
Managing Editor Emma Grange
Managing Art Editor Vicky Short
Publishing Director Mark Searle

Packaged for DK by Amazing15
Editor Martin Eden
Designers Martin Stiff and Marcus Scudamore

First published in Great Britain in 2023 by Dorling Kindersley Limited
DK, One Embassy Gardens, 8 Viaduct Gardens, London SW11 7BW
A Penguin Random House Company

The authorised representative in the EEA is
Dorling Kindersley Verlag GmbH. Arnulfstr. 124, 80636 Munich, Germany

Page design copyright © 2023 Dorling Kindersley Limited
DK, a Division of Penguin Random House LLC
10 9 8 7 6 5 4 3 2 1
001–334773–Sep/2023

A CIP catalogue record for this book is available from the British Library.
ISBN 978-0-2416-1061-9

Printed and bound in China

ACKNOWLEDGEMENTS
DK would like to thank the comic book artists whose talent made this book possible; Melanie Scott for her text and
expertise; Benjamin Harper and Josh Anderson at Warner Bros., and Benjamin Le Clear, Mike Pallotta, Leah Tuttle,
Hank Manfra, Steve Sonn, Doug Prinzivalli and Michael McCalister at DC for vital help and advice; Elizabeth Cook
for additional editing and coordination; Amazing15 for packaging; and Kayla Dugger for proofreading.

For the curious
www.dk.com

MIX
Paper | Supporting
responsible forestry
FSC™ C018179

This book was made with Forest
Stewardship Council™ certified
paper – one small step in DK's
commitment to a sustainable future.
**For more information go to
www.dk.com/our-green-pledge**